Stark Raving Obedience

Isaiah Kallman
Ted Kallman

PRAYERSHOP
PUBLISHING

Terre Haute, Indiana

PrayerShop Publishing is the publishing arm of Harvest Prayer Ministries and the Church Prayer Leaders Network. Harvest Prayer Ministries exists to transform lives through teaching prayer.

Its online prayer store, www.prayershop.org, has more than 600 prayer resources available for purchase.

Third Edition

Scripture quotations, unless otherwise indicated, are taken from the New American Standard Bible®, copyright © 1960, 1962, 1963, 1968, 1971, 1972, 1973, 1975, 1977, 1995 by The Lockman Foundation. Used by permission.

Scripture labeled AMP is taken from the Amplified® Bible, Copyright © 1954, 1958, 1962, 1964, 1965, 1987 by the Lockman Foundation. Used by permission.

Scripture labeled NIV is taken from the Holy Bible, NEW INTERNATIONAL VERSION®. Copyright © 1973, 1978, 1984 International Bible Society. All rights reserved throughout the world. Used by permission of International Bible Society.

Scripture labeled NKJV is taken from the New King James Version®. Copyright © 1982 by Thomas Nelson, Inc. Used by permission. All rights reserved.

Scriptured labeled KJV is taken from King James Version.

DISCLAIMER
Authors and Publisher have used their best efforts in making this book, including all endnotes and quotations, as accurate as possible. In the event that any inaccuracy has occurred, this is unintentional, and we apologize for such oversights.

ISBN: 9781935012092
Library of Congress Control Number: 2009904213

Printed in the United States of America

1 2 3 4 5 6 7 8 9 10 | 2016 2015 2014 2013 2012 2011 2010 2009

Acknowledgments

We printed a few hundred copies of an earlier draft several years ago. This was done to gather feedback and ideas for refining the book. Sale of the limited edition helped us fund the creation of the next version. Bill Noordyk of Noordyk Business Equipment in Grand Rapids offered to print these books for us to assist in getting the message out. Thank you Bill for your belief in this message and your help in getting the first draft done and on the street. These editions paved the way until PrayerShop Publishing picked up this book to make it available to a wider audience. We are grateful to all who have believed in this message and worked to put it in the hands of others.

Special thanks to my (Ted) wife, Claudia, who has lived this listening, relational walk since she was a child and has fed our understanding every step of this relationship with God's heart. Also, thanks to the many people who have given us feedback and comments over the years for their insights and encouragement.

Contents

Introduction

Welcome. This book has been requested for many years, and we are now finally publishing it. About five years ago I asked my son Isaiah, an aspiring young writer to help me with the compilation of the material and to add some of his own experiences as well. His writing effort has brought us to this point. Actually, to be more accurate, I was praying one morning and asking God how in the world I was going to find the time to move this project along, and He said to me "Your son is a writer. Ask him to help." Here is an interesting concept: I was listening to God on how to complete the book on listening prayer and He directed my steps and gave me the solution.

The result is that you will see my stories and teachings mingled with my wife Claudia's and Isaiah's as well. My other children, Ben, James, and Etta, added to the conversations of this book from our Sunday listening prayer times (a legacy that continues to this day) and the ever-changing ebb and flow of our family life. The chorus of these voices together have formed the basis for this book. The written voice (I) is Isaiah's, but the content comes from all of us.

Francis Schaeffer wrote a book and video series in the 1970s titled *How Should We Then Live?* It was a call to consider how we, as people who believe in God and the Christian faith, should orient our lives to most effectively impact our culture for the kingdom of God. The question is still relevant today and this book is a reflection of the path God has taken our family down in answering that question.

For us it has become *stark raving obedience.*

It really started with Claudia, my wife of nearly thirty-five years. Her relationship with God has been intimate and conversational from her earliest memories. Early in our marriage she would mention things that God had shown her or direction that she knew was from God, and I would blow it off. Unfortunately at that time in my life my primary spiritual gifts were anger, bluntness, insensitivity, religious arrogance, and stupidity. These are not particularly excellent gifts and will not be found in the Bible. They are actually from the "other team" spiritually, but they were a part of my life. I did not, hopefully, blow off Claudia's insights out of spite or a lack of love for her. It was simply that if something did not make logical sense to me, then I would not even consider it. I now believe that we missed many blessings and ministry opportunities as a result of my logic filters and unwillingness to hear God.

Forgive me Lord.

In 1993 I was given a book written by Mary Geegh called *God Guides.* It was a little self-published work written by a missionary from Holland, Michigan, who served with the Reformed Church in America in India for more than thirty-eight years. It is a series of short stories about how God taught her to listen for direction from the Holy Spirit to resolve problems in ministry and life situations and how, when that direction was obeyed miracles resulted. Reprints of this book are available on our website www.hearinggod.org.

When I first read the book, I thought *I do not know anyone who lives this way.* The fact that Claudia lived this life had completely escaped my notice even after reading the book. I guess it takes some of us a little longer to get things than others. Did I mention the gift of stupidity?

Regardless of my past inability to see listening as vital to a deep relationship with the living God, the book struck me as true, so I began to listen.

The first time I tried to "listen" to God it was hard. Sitting at the desk in my office at home, the noise of all the lists of things to do at work and home flew into my head and would not go away. I finally said, "God, I am not leaving here until you say something so You might as well speak." I do not know how long I waited, and I do not know how long I would have stayed but I did have a tenacious intention that I was not leaving until I heard from God.

After a period of time I heard the thought in my spirit "I love you." A dry twig snapped inside of me, and I wept for more than an hour. It just poured out. I was not prone to crying prior to that day, but when I heard that thought something broke. I knew it was God. I knew it was real. My performance-based ideas of how the Christian life should be lived began to die that day. Thus started my journey in a relationship with God that I had no idea was available.

I began to listen on a regular basis, and it changed my life. I started to pray this way with Claudia, and it changed our marriage. We started to pray this way with the kids, and it changed our home. We started to pray this way with our small group, and it changed our lives. It changed my work.

It changed everything.

Our prayer is that God will open the ears of your heart and deepen your relationship as a result of our story. I know that if you seek Him with your whole heart He will be found.

Our hope is that this book will stir up in you a hunger for the

God who will be found and begin to nudge you toward listening and obeying Him in ways you never have in the past. Also, as you begin to push through your walls of discomfort and dance with the living God, the experience will cause spiritual ripples to emanate from your life that will have impact for generations.

Welcome to *Stark Raving Obedience.* —Ted Kallman

Preface

People talk to God all the time. Whether it's someone praying for friends and family, at the dinner table, or at a baseball game, talking to God is pretty ordinary. On the other hand, tell someone that God talks to you, and they might look at you like you ought to be locked up and psychoanalyzed.

It's hard to deny that people are searching for something in their lives. Dating services try to provide people with intimacy. Some people drink to numb their pain, an attempt at healing their wounds if only temporarily. I (Isaiah) remember a professor in college claiming that television was a way for people to have a community experience, a nation of people experiencing the same "events" while sitting alone in their homes. Something exists in every man and woman that longs for *something,* even if they can't explain what they long for. I know that lots of people are just searching for answers, and many of them are seeking God for those answers, even if they don't realize it.

But how can a person ask God a question when they don't believe that He'll tell them the answer? How can God give direction if He doesn't communicate with us? A person might argue that God speaks to us in the Bible. True, but maybe I want to know if I should take a job overseas, or maybe I want to know how to reconcile a relationship with a family member. Personal stuff. Sometimes uncomfortable and complicated stuff. I believe that God wants to direct us and answer *our* questions personally, not just the deep questions of mankind as a whole.

How can you have a personal relationship with someone who isn't personal? We say the words "personal relationship" a lot in the church, but I don't know if the church always does a good job of explaining (or understanding) a real personal relationship with Jesus Christ.

A few years ago, I joined the Rachael Leigh Cook fan club after watching the movie *Josie and the Pussycats*. I saw all of her movies. I read her biographical information. I read all the news updates, participated in a few of the fan club chats, and sent her a two-and-a-half-page fan letter. Even after all of that, I don't think anyone in their right mind would say that I had a personal relationship with Rachael Leigh Cook.

At a young age, I was told that if I read my Bible, went to church or youth groups, and prayed to God (talked at Him), then I had a healthy, personal relationship with Him. Now I know better. It's good to do all those things, but it's not enough. It's not personal. The only way to have a personal relationship with anybody is to talk with them, to build trust and have a history with them. Is that possible with an immaterial God? I know now that it is.

I am not an expert. Nobody has all the answers. This book doesn't even *begin* to have all of the answers. My family and I have gone through the last sixteen years of our lives learning how to listen to God, and we've come closer to Him than we thought at all possible. But we will never know everything there is to know about God's relationship with mankind. We'll continue to amend and clarify things as God continues to teach us more about Himself. But a person may as well say they know the number of infinity, or have named every one of the cells in their body, if they say they know all about God. In this little book, I just want to communicate this: how to reach a *greater* level of intimacy with God. —Isaiah Kallman

A Very True Story

A woman in mid-Michigan had just begun to listen for the voice of God when she prayed. Driving home one day, she felt something in her spirit say, "Stop in the 7-Eleven and go stand on your head next to the pop machine." Was that God? To her, it felt more like some bad cold cuts in her lunch, or some sort of short circuit in her brain. Then she heard that internal voice again, "Stop in the 7-Eleven and go stand on your head next to the pop machine."

By now she could see the 7-Eleven, but she was determined to continue on her way home. God didn't make insane requests like that, especially not to people like her. Old Testament prophets and ascetic Nazarenes, maybe, but not normal people. This time, the nudge had urgency. "Go back to the 7-Eleven and stand on your head next to the pop machine."

She turned her car around and parked in front of the 7-Eleven. There were no other cars. At least no one would stare at her, she thought. When she entered, she saw a young man standing behind the counter, and the woman wished that he would go into the back room to stock some things. She walked over next to the pop machine, stood on her head, and . . . nothing happened.

Weren't the heavens supposed to have torn open to the sound of angel choirs singing because she obeyed? What gives?

The woman began to walk out, and the young man behind the counter stopped her. "Excuse me, why did you just do that?"

Okay, how does one explain this in a spiritually relevant way? "Ah yes, I was driving home, communing with the God of the universe, the Maker of heaven and earth, and He said to me, 'Oh woman of faith and power . . . go thou to the 7-Eleven and stand upon thy head by the pop machine!'" Does that sound normal? Does it sound sane? Does it even sound like God? No, it sounds stupid.

She told him to please just forget about it. "I'm sorry to have bothered you. I'm a little embarrassed. I think I'll just leave."

He insisted, "No, wait, I have to know why you did that." Then he pulled a gun out from under the counter. "A few minutes ago, I had this gun in my mouth. My life isn't worth living, and I was going to kill myself. At the last moment, I gave God one more chance. I said, 'God, if You are real, why don't You send somebody in here and have them stand on their head by the pop machine.' So I really need to know why you did that. Could you tell me about your God?"

So, was that God?

How do you know if it was God?

Would you have obeyed?

CHAPTER 1

Contact

Signs of Life

"One of the greatest blessings a true believer has is to hear and know the voice of God. It is possible to hear God's voice today as certainly and clearly as did Abraham and Moses—as clearly as did Samuel and David—as clearly as did Paul, Peter, the apostles, and John on the isle of Patmos!"—David Wilkerson[1]

t all began with a prayer, at a time when I wasn't sure if I took prayer seriously. This particular prayer was in response to Psalm 42:1: "As the deer pants for the water brooks, so pants my soul for You, O God." As I read about David's thirst for God, I realized that even though I belonged to "the Jesus Christ Club" of Christianity, and believed myself a sold-out disciple because I did all the correct "church" things, and had once read the Bible the whole way through, I did not feel a desperate longing for God.

People often tell testimonies like this: "My life hit rock bottom, and I didn't know what to do. Then I found Jesus. Now I have all of this joy and peace and success." Well, it was only sort of like that for the Kallmans.

We had come to a bad place as a family when I was eleven years old. My brothers Ben and James got burned by people in the church and it seemed like they decided to break every rule the church tried to place on them. The family business had struggled, and we lived on the edge of financial failure. All of that strained Mom and Dad to heartbreaking points. I was intensely unhappy and hated myself. Once or twice I snuck into my brothers' world to see if drugs would make me happy. And of course they didn't. For me, faith was two parts habit and one part safety precaution. I knew I didn't want to go to hell, so I became a Christian, but devotion to a religion didn't seem to fix anything. I felt like I was living in hell already.

At the time, I didn't know that my father, Ted, and I were in the same place spiritually. We knew that we had accepted Christ and tried to live our lives according to His teachings, but God was this distant being to whom we paid tribute with routine. Prayer, reading the Bible, attending church, helping with church activities, Bible camp, charity, mission trips that suspiciously looked like vacations. Witnessing never seemed to do any good back then because people could probably tell that I wasn't so sure about God myself.

A part of our family's routine was to spend time together on Sunday nights. Usually it meant pizza and a movie. One Sunday night, we didn't have pizza or a movie. My brothers became angry and asked why we were just sitting around the living room with nothing to do.

"We're going to pray," my mother answered.

I figured that one of our family members or friends was in trouble, because that seemed like the only time we sat together as a family to pray. Dad said that nobody was hurt or anything. "We want to teach you children something that your mom and I have been learning together."

Ben and James looked like they wanted to leave but knew that it would cause more trouble than they were willing to make. My sister, Etta, often hiding silently behind our couch, took it all in. I remember feeling confused and intrigued. I knew how to talk to God. Every Sunday school kid knew what prayer was, but Mom and Dad had just explained that we could listen to God talk back. It sounded like a thought, but the thought was sometimes God talking to us.

So this is usually the part of that testimony where God changes our lives and everything gets better. The family magically alters into this perfect home and all of us get along and sunshine pours out of our fingertips.

That didn't quite happen. God began to show us the areas in our lives that needed to change, and there were a lot of areas that needed change. Over time, God sometimes asked us to do strange and uncomfortable things. But when we met on Sunday night and asked God to talk to us, all of the problems we faced couldn't diminish my excitement. I had actually met God, and He met me.

The preacher in the punk band had it right.

My former pastor used to have a rock-and-roll band called Big Fil. Their "big hit" was a song called "I'm Not Your Grandpa." In the song, God spoke to His people, asking them when they would realize that He was right in the middle of their lives. He wasn't some crazy old man that lived in the attic with flowing white hair. It's a great song. I own all of their records.

But I digress.

The point is that God wants a personal relationship with us. You've heard that before, right? I mean, He wants to be able to walk with us in the cool of the evening and talk with us, just like He did with Adam and Eve in the Garden of Eden. He wants to be able to meet with us on mountains and talk directly to us like He did with Moses. This same God tore the veil in the temple from top to bottom when Jesus died. Man and God can interact freely, no priest required.

I've told lots of people that this book is all about prayer, but it's really about knowing God. When we hear His voice and obey, then see amazing things come from that obedience, we learn to trust Him. We can approach God with confidence; we can *seek* Him and actually *find* Him.

I'm going to talk about sheer madness. I'm going to talk about the best thing that ever happened to me.

Henry Ford once said whether you believe you can or cannot, you are correct. Despite its self-centered bent, there is some truth to it. Before we begin anything here, you have to understand: If you don't believe that God can or will speak to you, then you are absolutely right. This isn't a case of mind over matter, that the more affirmation you give something the truer it becomes. I'm saying that anyone can hear, but you have to make it a point to listen.

If you're somebody who really believes that the Bible is the true Word of God, that the Word is unchanging, that God is the same "yesterday, today, and forever" (Hebrews 13:8), why wouldn't you believe He still speaks?

The book *The Lives of the Desert Fathers* gives a record of miracles, healings, signs, and wonders that were prevalent in the lives of monks along the Nile from about AD 100 to about AD 450. It includes a direct translation of *The Historia Monachorum In Aegypto*, which tells the stories of these men and their intense pursuit of God. Listening while in prayer was a significant part of their walk.[2]

In his book *Surprised by the Voice of God*, Jack Deere details instances where the early Reformers heard direction from the Spirit and acted in obedience, and how God moved miraculously. This book also cites Jonathan Edwards and Charles Hadden Spurgeon with similar instances.[3]

A. W. Tozer in his classic book *The Pursuit of God* describes the ongoing speaking nature of God in the chapter "The Speaking Voice."[4]

The problem I have in teaching people about hearing God's voice comes in the matter of incontrovertible proof. I'm not sure I could come up with a list of bibliographical sources that would satisfy critical minds. I can only present the best information that I have and give accounts of experience.

But they aren't all just my experiences, or my family's, or of people unknown to the public. I've already mentioned Jack Deere's book, *Surprised y the Voice of God.* At the beginning of the book, Deere tells a story of God supernaturally speaking to him. A student came to speak with Deere about a paper, and the Holy Spirit told Deere that this student struggled with pornography. Deere describes his reaction. "*What is happening to me?* I thought. *There is no way this student is into pornography. I must be making this up.* But why would I make up something I thought to be an impossibility?" When Deere asked if the student was struggling with pornography, the young man began to confess and repent of many different sins, including his addiction to pornography. Later that night, the student found Deere and exclaimed, "I'm a new person!"

I believe this all began with Deere relentlessly seeking God's voice. "For months, I had been praying for God to speak to me like this, asking Him to impart to me supernatural knowledge about people so that I might minister to them more effectively."[5]

My high school Algebra teacher had an annoying habit of saying the same two phrases whenever I asked him a question, "it's in the book" or "it's in your notes." I used to wonder why, then, I had a teacher at all. I should have just been able to read the book and look at the notes and understand how to find "X." But I didn't understand. I needed him to sit down with me and go over whatever impeded my comprehension. I remember muttering to myself, "No, it's in your head."

Growing up in my church, Sunday school teachers and youth pastors told me that God said everything He needed to say in the Bible, so He doesn't have to talk anymore. I don't buy that. I don't think they were lying to me. They just didn't know how to listen to God, so they assumed He had finished talking. I do believe that the Bible is God's word, and that it is fully true. I don't believe that it's exhaustive, though, because that would mean the eternal God limited the whole of His being to a book with a beginning and an end. John said it himself in his gospel, "And there are also many other things which Jesus did, which if they were written in detail, I suppose that even the world itself would not contain the books that would be written" (Jn. 21:25).

In John 16:7-15, Jesus tells His disciples that the Holy Spirit will come to guide them after He has gone. He says that the Holy Spirit "will guide you into all truth," and that the Spirit "will convict the world concerning sin and righteousness and judgment." The guidance of the Holy Spirit was not exclusively for the apostles, and there was a need for guidance beyond the words written in the Scriptures. Otherwise, Jesus would have left His disciples with Abraham's words from the parable of the Rich Man and Lazarus in Luke 16:29, "But Abraham said, 'They have Moses and the Prophets; let them hear them.'" In other words, "It's in the book. It's in your notes."

But even if that were the case, the Bible has no life apart from the Spirit's illumination. In Greek, there are two different words for "Word." The first is *logos*, which refers to the written and spoken word. The other is *rhema*, which refers specifically to the spoken word. Now, I have only studied a little bit of the Greek language (very, very little), and I don't claim to have scholarly credentials, but I take it to mean this: When I read the Bible, I read words (*logos*), but when that word takes on personal meaning, and I feel the Holy Spirit speaking directly to me through the words, that's *rhema*. *Logos* is written and *rhema* is spoken or breathed. I read *logos,* but hear and understand *rhema*.

In the Catholic Church, some believers follow a practice of praying the Scriptures aloud and meditating on them. There are two ways that this form of prayer is practiced, one good and the other highly suspect, but I'll talk of that later.

Even with the Word of God we need to hear His voice to gain true wisdom and understanding. If we study the Bible apart from the Spirit, we can have knowledge of the Word, but not wisdom. Wisdom can only come from having a relationship with the living God. No *rhema*, no wisdom.

In a letter to one of his closest friends, Francis Schaeffer discussed the "moment by moment" reality of God and how it applied to their faith and mission.

> I am not thinking of this in some "mystical" area where God becomes an abstraction, but in the strenuously practical areas of history in which we walk. If we would only allow the Agent of the Trinity, the Holy Spirit, to lead each individual instead of living in the areas of rules

which are man-made and quite apart from the absolutes laid down in Scripture. If only we would be willing to have Christ be the true Head, and be willing for the exotic leadership of the Holy Spirit in our individual and corporate lives—rather than stagnifying the Holy Spirit's leadership of yesterday, as seen in the lives of other men who lived in different historic circumstances, when the infinite eye of God would see today's history as requiring a slightly different or radically different approach; or even stagnifying how the Holy Spirit's leading of us today be what it was a year ago, when our historic circumstance is always in a flux?[6]

Here, according to Schaeffer, to claim that God has no need or desire to guide us in our present day is to "stagnify" the Holy Spirit. It renders His power ineffective, and if it were true, would make me wonder if His love for me were secondary.

So what am I saying?

First, God still communicates directly to people. There are examples of this throughout the Bible, Christian history, and our present day.

Second, our belief impacts our ability to hear God.

Third, as the Word says in Jeremiah 29:13, if we pursue God with our whole heart, He will be found.

We can hear through our relationships, through reading the Bible, through dreams and visions, and through the physical world we live in. More often than not, though, God speaks through thoughts. So let's look more in-depth at the sources of thoughts in our heads.

CHAPTER 2

Listening
The Voices We Hear

"I do dearly wish the Lord would give His revelations more emphatically than He does, but He doesn't—not generally. I have taken to saying that He speaks in a 'whis,' which is half a whisper. That means He expects us to take action on the basis of what seems to us woefully insignificant guidance."—Mike Flynn, Episcopal Rector[7]

od still speaks to people today. I've heard Him. People all over the globe have heard Him. When I tell people this, one of the first questions I have to answer is, "Just how do I hear God?" If they accept that God does speak to us today, many of them go on to ask, "How do I know it is Him?"

Good question.

Most of the time when we get a thought in our heads that makes us pause and think, we assume that it is just our thought. If it doesn't make sense, we dismiss it and move on. Back in the Kallman's living room, that Sunday night in 1994, I learned that all thoughts are not my thoughts. There are in fact many sources for the thoughts that cruise through our brains. We need to learn how to discern where they come from, what to pay attention to, and what to ignore.

Not all thoughts are our thoughts.

We are in our own heads. I mean, we do have our own thoughts bouncing around in our minds. Many people have sat down to listen while they pray and have heard a laundry list of things to do like, "Clean the basement, don't forget about that meeting, you've got to cook your own dinner." In my case, at least, these are usually my own thoughts distracting me from focusing on God. C. S. Lewis, in his book *Perelandra*, explained this voice so simply. "There is a chattering part of the mind which continues, until it is corrected, to chatter on even in the holiest of places."[8]

But not all thoughts are our thoughts. A few Scriptures lead us to this conclusion. Mark 7:21-23 indicates that from our own heart come all kinds of bad stuff, evil thoughts, pride, deceit, and so on. Our own fallen nature can be the source of a thought even if we've accepted Jesus as our Savior. If you don't believe me, refer to the apostle Paul's account of the war within himself in Romans 7:13-25. At one point he tries to explain the duality of his bodily nature and the Spirit of God in him. And at best it sounds confusing. The italics here are mine. "For what I am doing, I do not understand. For what I will to do, that I do not practice; but what I hate, that I do. If, then, I do what I will not to do, I agree with the law that *it is* good." Even though I have accepted Christ, I'm not perfect, and my own mind can ramble on while I listen for God's voice.

Silencing the voice of your flesh isn't clearing out your ability to think, wrestle, argue, or question. It means you've asked God to silence the part of your old, sinful nature that would answer your own questions for you by shouting out your desires.

Other people could speak and influence our thoughts. I call this "the voice of the world." When I pray, at times I hear my peers in my thoughts, what they would say about my situation. "You're not actually going to do that, are you? Don't be an idiot." Although God uses people to speak truth into our lives, our families and culture place their own standards on us. Sometimes God wants us to obey Him despite what society would think.

Sometimes, we have heard something said to us, and those words we hear become our natural response. Imagine a parent telling a child, "See, that's what happens when you get your own way," or "You're so stupid, you'll never amount to anything." Now, that child could grow up thinking they should never get their own way, or else something bad will happen. They might get a bad grade on a pop quiz and think that they're a failure. Even years later, they hear the words their parent said to them when they were a child.

Dad and I call those thoughts "old tapes playing." It's like that mix tape of Jermaine Jackson "hits" buried in the crease of your car's passenger seat. An old girlfriend made it for you decades ago, and you don't see it to think about it, but every now and again it resurfaces. Then it's 1983 all over again, and you still hate it.

The words you might hear in your own thoughts, those "tapes," are usually lies. And I don't mean things like, "don't eat stuff that you find on the floor." That's good advice, believe me. I'm referring to words like, "You're such a disappointment" or "never trust anybody." Those tapes will continue to play in our minds until we silence them.

The enemy is also a source for thoughts. We see this in John 13:2, where the devil "put into the heart of Judas Iscariot, the son of Simon, to betray him." The Amplified Bible translation makes an even stronger statement. "Satan placed the thought into Judas to betray Christ" (AMP). Satan is a roaring lion roaming about seeking whom he may devour, and he will attack our thoughts as a means to accomplish his destruction (1 Pet. 5:8).

A few years ago, I told my friend, Luke, how he could listen to God when praying. He tried listening to God later that day and heard the words, "You must die." He sensed that this was not a "living sacrifice" type of death (Rom. 12:1) but that it was a threat and it really scared him. When I called him later that day, I could hear the strain in his voice, "I think I'm going to die." While it is true that we will all die someday, I couldn't believe that those words came from God. It sounded more like a spiritual attack causing fear and stress. We dealt with it by praying, renouncing the lie and replacing it with truth. After we prayed, peace came back into Luke's spirit.

We don't have to sit around and take Satan's harassment, though. We don't have to second-guess ourselves all the time wondering if our own desires are driving our thoughts, or if old tapes are playing in our minds. Read this next verse carefully. I've added the italics. "For though we walk in the flesh, we do not war according to the flesh, for the weapons of our warfare are not of the flesh, but divinely powerful for the destruction of fortresses. We are destroying speculations and every lofty thing raised up against the knowledge of God, and we are *taking every thought captive to the obedience of Christ*" (2 Cor. 10:3-5). From this word, I came to understand that the enemy whispers lies into my mind, but I have the authority to bind the voices, silence them, and place them under God's control.

There is another voice, the voice of the Holy Spirit. James writes, "If anyone lacks wisdom let him ask God, who gives to all men generously and without reproach, and it will be given to him" (Jas. 1:5). In John 16:13, the Word says, "But when he, the Spirit of truth, comes, he will guide you into all the truth." And later, John 10:27 says, "My sheep hear My voice and I know them and they follow Me." Although there is a cultural relevance to this verse, Jesus speaking to people familiar with flocks of sheep, I also believe that we can hear God's voice call out to us (I feel that I should point out that this verse says "They hear . . ." not "They might hear . . ."). I had to know that the voice of the Lord called out to me, otherwise how could I have chosen to follow Him? I made the decision to follow by the leading of the Holy Spirit, my guide.

Not every bird is a duck.

My sister's second favorite word in the English language is "duck." "Czechoslovakia" takes the number one spot, but according to her, "Duck is just satisfying to say."

Imagine the talk in my family when my nephew, Wesley, chose "duck" as his first word. And he would say it with much gusto, as if he also found it satisfying to say. It didn't take long for James and his wife to notice that aside from "mamamama" and "dadadada," "duck" was the only word that Wesley spoke for months.

They were concerned at first, until one day when Wesley had a picture book of birds in front of him. He turned each page, pointed at the eagle or pelican or heron, and said, "Mamama, duck!" At least he understood that a duck was a bird. But to Wesley, every bird was a duck.

A few years ago, a girl I sat next to in a college class asked me to explain the subject of this book. I told her about hearing God's voice and the amazing things that happen when we obey Him and build a relationship with Him.

"Oh. Are you a spiritualist?"

Instead of admitting that I didn't know exactly what she meant, I said, "It's a fine line." She frowned at me, and the conversation pretty much ended there.

Again, a girl from South Carolina began corresponding with me about my band, Vigilantes. When she asked me what I did outside of the band, I told her about *Stark Raving Obedience*. She replied, "So would you say you're more spiritual than religious?" I told her that she could put it that way, because I believed that direct communication with God on the spiritual level was more important than devotion to a list of dos and don'ts.

"I think I'm like that, too," she said. Then the conversation shifted toward Buddha and Carl Jung.

Dad and I have noticed a lot of people speaking a similar language when they talk about how all gods are God, how all spirits are holy, and so on. They use almost the exact same words for mantra and channeling that we use for recognizing the Holy Spirit's voice through listening prayer.

Dealing with the Problem

There are three ways a person can react to this problem. The first way is to dismiss it altogether, like the girl that I went to college with who frowned at me. Sometimes people hear our stories of listening and compare it with things like *centering prayer* or *contemplative prayer*. Even though the descriptions of centering and contemplative prayer are similar, these are not the same as listening prayer. While there is some good in those concepts, there are also dangers. And because of the dangers, some write off those practices altogether.

A few years ago, some people had invited me to visit a church on the east side of Grand Rapids. I had a major crush on one of the girls, so of course I agreed to attend the next Sunday morning. The church introduced a guest speaker. This woman had a masters of this and doctorate of that, having received a grant to study the history of prayer and religious tradition.

At first, I was eager to hear what she had to say. After all, prayer has been a major focus of my spiritual life and I expected to learn something. The woman began to teach the history of a Catholic tradition called *Lectio Divina*, which is a form of praying the Scriptures and allowing the Holy Spirit to open your understanding to those verses. I had heard of this before, no problem. Next, she spoke of contemplative prayer and the works of a man named Thomas Merton. Within minutes I felt my insides turn. The words she spoke sounded all right, but something else lay underneath her teaching that troubled my spirit. My suspicions were justified when she began to say that this prayer helped her realize the sacredness within her and that she could be like God.

Now, this didn't sound like she meant "Christlike," where Christians try to walk by the power of the Holy Spirit with the humble recognition that they will not be Christs themselves. It sounded more like the deception of the serpent in Genesis 3 when it tempted Eve to eat the forbidden fruit. "For God knows that in the day you eat from it your eyes will be opened, and you will be like God, knowing good and evil" (v. 5). I wanted to stand up and say something. I wanted to do a lot of things to stop her from talking, but I didn't. What would the girl sitting next to me think if I did such a thing?

The lesson went on to teach on centering prayer. The woman wanted the congregation to practice this form of prayer by repeating Psalm 46:10 from the King James Bible. The whole verse is, "Be still, and know that I am God: I will be exalted among the heathen, I will be exalted in the earth." I had another check in my spirit when she immediately cut out the second half of the verse. I don't even believe she mentioned it. And yet, the second half of the verse deals with God's glory throughout the earth. That's the part about praise. It gives the first half its context. Another translation says to stop striving and know that God is God. God is God and we are not.

She had everyone repeat it quietly to themselves as she prayed in a soft, breathy voice. The whole time I prayed a covering over the people hearing, that the Holy Spirit would guard them from the counterfeit and speak the truth of God's Word into their hearts. The woman began to cut out words one by one, beginning with "God," until she was repeating the word "know." When she came to the last part of her prayer, I felt like I was choking.

After the service, I approached the woman and began asking questions and telling her about my own experience with prayer. "It's not a mystical, otherworldly prayer. It's not separated from the day-to-day experience. Mine is conversational and personal prayer." Then I began to offer scriptures as support of listening prayer. The woman didn't respond. She stared at me, and at times gave me a condescending smile. I saw that the conversation wasn't going anywhere, so I thanked her for her time and met my friends outside.

They were visibly uncomfortable. Some of them said they didn't want to think about it anymore. I asked them if I could join them for lunch. "I want to talk to all of you. The woman inside, she was close to the truth, but then went in the wrong direction. But you can interact with God in prayer. You can hear and know His voice, and I want to tell you how." At a large cafeteria table, I spoke to those college students about listening prayer, making sure to involve as much Scripture as possible. We are not supposed to base our faith on tradition, I said, but Scripture. Our relationship with God is a personal one based on the Word, not a mystical and incommunicable experience with "the divine" to become divine ourselves.

This story grieves me. Not only do people buy into counterfeits of God's voice too easily, but others see the result of listening to a lie and reject the truth along with it. I mean, it's like a person witnessing a devastating car crash and refusing to ever ride in an automobile. Or if the person knows that some movies are full of violence, sex, foul language, or any material they might consider offensive, then decides to avoid the movie theater altogether. How many times have you heard people say that they don't believe in Christianity because of the hypocrisy in the church? I heard three girls talking about it last weekend. Some people see the pride and hypocrisy in Christians that doesn't go along with Scripture, and as a result reject Jesus outright. You might try to tell them that the hypocritical and condemning attitude isn't Christlike. And you might tell them that it's unreasonable to reject Christianity based on the shortcomings or failures of certain people. But to some people every bird is a duck.

The second way that people can respond to the idea of connecting with the spiritual realm is to believe it's all good and true, and find themselves far away from Jesus, from the God of the Bible, from the Holy Spirit. The problem is that there are a lot of voices out to confuse and distract us from hearing the voice of the Holy Spirit. And when a person begins to take in all the voices that they hear, I notice how universalistic their view of faith becomes. "Oh man, it's all God. It's just how you hear Him."

This is only partially true. God does speak to us in ways that we hear Him, but not everything we hear is God. Just because every duck is a bird doesn't mean that every bird is a duck. Just because

God speaks to us in spirit doesn't mean that every spirit that speaks to us is God.

The Devil by nature is a deceiver. He will take the truth and alter it so slightly that the differences become almost imperceptible on the surface. At the risk of sounding cliché, think about counterfeit money. A person who wants to convince someone else that they have legitimate money won't have a twenty dollar bill with purple octopi squirting patriot missiles behind an American flag . . . and so on. They're going to try to copy the real thing as closely as possible so that the person taking the money doesn't notice the difference. And yet, with counterfeits, there's always a difference when you line it up with the real thing.

In fact, I've heard that Canadian Mounties study and memorize every detail of their legitimate paper money. That way, when they come across a counterfeit bill, they will recognize the flaws. Knowing the true nature of something takes experience and discipline. Just as those Mounties learn to recognize the truth before the false, chefs train their palate to recognize distinct flavors in their food.

This leads me to the third way that we can look at communicating with God on a spiritual level, by looking at the end result the voice brings. It's the idea that a grape vine doesn't grow apples and an apple tree doesn't grow burritos. You know a tree by the fruit that it produces (Lk. 6:44). When we pray and listen, we can understand that although God does speak to us, lying voices are also speaking. And if we have diligently studied Scripture, we can line up whatever voice we hear with the Bible and ask if it really is the voice of God.

Journaling

When I was still pretty young, I remember struggling with the idea that the Bible was God's Word, but written by lots of men. Who was the author, then? The men who wrote it down on paper or the God who spoke and inspired the words? It's now my understanding that God revealed Himself to men and inspired every word they wrote.

But any discerning reader can see that the writing style changes depending on the person writing the individual books within the Bible. Paul's letters read with a poetic grace. Ezra wrote from the perspective of a priest. Luke had the attention to detail fitting to his profession as a physician. Many of the prophets were singers and their works flow like lyrical poetry. God spoke to each of the writers in a way the writers could understand.

I have a dear friend named Jeremy Rush who often sees odd and vivid pictures when God speaks to him. Seriously, he once saw a picture of a cat floating in outer space when we were praying at church. My sister, Etta, used to hear God speak with Michael W. Smith song lyrics. It's not always just conversational words, and it's not always the same kind of conversation. Even though I have a relationship with the same God as Etta and Rush, we don't have the same kinds of conversations.

For several years, I've tried to write down my conversations with God. I first got the idea from the book *God Guides*, because author Mary Geegh used journaling of her thoughts to remember and confirm what she heard with what other people had heard.[9] In *Dialogue with God*, Mark Virkler wrote down his conversations with God for similar reasons.[10]

I place some emphasis on writing down the words that I hear when I listen to God because it slows down the rhythm of my brain. The simple act of writing my questions and God's answers, the dialogue, filters out much of the white noise in my life. Journaling also allows me to look back on my growth in God. I see the first instances of listening where He said "I love you," and "Do you trust Me?" I read the promises of the past that He fulfilled, whether I realized it or not.

In other cases, writing down what I hear from God also gives me more resolve to obey what He asks of me. It keeps an accountability. On Christmas Eve, I heard in prayer that I was supposed to go on a road trip. I asked God when and where. He gave me a specific time frame (the beginning of March) and told me each city I should visit. I wrote this all down.

I had made commitments with my band at the time to write a record between January and April, which I was also directed in prayer to do. So I assumed that I would follow that direction in prayer and forget about the early March road trip. There were also the circumstances of having no money for a trip, or a reliable car to drive around the country.

Two weeks before March, one of the band members suggested we take a break from writing. I asked when he'd like to take this time off, and he said, "I was thinking March second to March tenth." Suddenly, I remembered what I had heard in prayer back in December. I checked my prayer journal, and sure enough, I was told to leave the first week of March.

That weekend, I told my parents that I had heard God tell me to go on this road trip. "I guess I have the time, but I don't have enough money, and my car would never make it."

Dad chuckled and said, "I was paid this week by one of my clients, and I heard in prayer this morning that you were supposed to get a percentage of that money."

Then Mom said that thanks to the paycheck, she was able to have her car serviced. "You can borrow it for the trip."

God had told me to go, then provided the time, money, and transportation. My prayer journal reminded me of when and where I was supposed to go on a trip that I had dismissed for other plans. Dad's prayer journal reminded him that he was supposed to give me a certain amount of money, which covered all of my costs by the end of the trip.

Journaling isn't essential to listening. It can, however, help the process of learning how to listen. I'll also write down my own questions and responses to God in parentheses so I know how the conversation flowed at both ends. It's funny how often I'm arguing with Him in those parentheses, too. There are some days in which I hear something in prayer, but it doesn't look right on paper, so I'll ask for confirmation. And when there are so many kinds of voices trying to speak to me, I sometimes need that confirmation.

CHAPTER 3

Earplugs
Impediments to Hearing God's Voice

e all sin. Nobody has it all figured out. Even though we make mistakes, God still loves us and guides us. As author Andrew Murray puts it, "The Lord does not demand that we fulfill the law perfectly. All He requires is our childlike and wholehearted surrender to live as children with Him in obedience and truth."[11] Sometimes, though, our sin will get in the way of our communication with God so much that we cannot hear Him.

I call these sins "spiritual impediments." That might not be a very technical term. You might not hear it in seminary school. But I do know that sin can get in the way of our communication with God. Isaiah 59:1-2 says, and I'm paraphrasing here, that God is powerful enough to always hear and save, but sin separates us from Him and it disrupts our prayers. Again, in Psalm 66:17-18, "I cried to Him with my mouth, and He was extolled with my tongue. If I regard wickedness in my heart, the Lord will not hear." If sin keeps God from hearing us, I believe that this separation can certainly keep us from hearing Him.

But most of the time I look at spiritual impediments like earplugs, something that I stuck in my ears. And I'm not saying that you have to be completely free and clear of any and all mistakes before God will talk to you. I mean, I can still hear some things (with difficulty) when I wear earplugs. Besides, if we were perfect, then we probably wouldn't need God in the first place. I also know of many situations where God has spoken to people who don't have a relationship with Him at all, so I tread carefully on this ground. He invites us all to be with Him, we just have to say yes.

People often tell me, "I've prayed, but I haven't heard anything." In this case, I'll suggest that we get quiet and ask God to reveal any sin that might get in the way of God's voice. That may sound self-defeating, "God, I can't hear you. Tell me why I can't hear you." It sounds like a blind man asking for a lamp to read by, but I've found that the Holy Spirit will often bring something to mind. James 1:5 promises that God will give wisdom if we ask for it.

The main point here is we might have some sin that we've never dealt with from the past, or maybe sin that we've refused to give up to God, and sin will make it very difficult to have a good relationship with Him. It's like keeping any secret from a loved one. Sooner or later, the one little lie in the corner will spread until you can't be genuine with that person at all. A husband's hidden addiction to a substance, or depression, for example, will harm the intimacy with his wife. She might never know why her husband has withdrawn, but it will damage the marriage all the same.

Sometimes we don't even know what sin could be in the way of God talking to us. I've prayed with several people who asked God to reveal any sin in their lives that they needed to repent of, and He showed them something from their distant past that they'd completely forgotten. But, after they had repented and asked forgiveness, the barriers broke down and the relationship with God began to grow.

There is another step as well. In Matthew 12:43-45, Jesus taught,

> Now when the unclean spirit goes out of a man, it passes through waterless places seeking rest, and does not find it. Then it says, "I will return to my house from which I came"; and when it comes, it finds it unoccupied, swept, and put in order. Then it goes and takes along with it seven other spirits more wicked than itself, and they go in and live there; and the last state of that man becomes worse than the first. That is the way it will also be with this evil generation.

When we repent of sin and renounce our participation with it, it is important that we ask God to fill us with the presence of the Holy Spirit. You may ask, "But if I've asked Jesus into my heart, wouldn't the Holy Spirit already dwell in me?" Yes, but when you took on sin, and gave it a place in your heart, you essentially blocked God from that part of your life. You will have to ask Him to come in and dwell where that part of your life has been "cleaned out."

I wish I could write about all the different things that can get in the way of our relationship with God. I would like to help explain every little thing that may be wrong in your life and tell you how to fix it. But I don't know how to do that, and this isn't a self-help book.

The greatest book that I've read about spiritual impediments is *The Bondage Breaker* by Neil T. Anderson.[12] It spends a great deal of time detailing different sins, or agreements with lies, soul ties, unholy vows and oaths, etc. Anderson then steps the reader through a path of repentance. And really, that's the important thing—identifying the lie, rejecting the lie, repenting of the sin, and embracing the truth.

I will mention a few common things that get in the way of a healthy relationship with God, but I'll make it a short list. The point of this chapter isn't to rattle off every possible sin that has come between you and God, but to show you some of the ones that we might not realize in ourselves without addressing them. Ultimately, you ought to ask every day for God to reveal any sin that you have accepted so that you can repent and be free of it. As Psalm 139 says, the Lord knows you in every way, in all circumstances, in all places. There is nothing within you hidden from Him. At the end, the psalmist asks, "Search me, O God, and know my heart; try me and know my anxious thoughts; and see if there be any hurtful way in me, and lead me in the everlasting way" (vv. 23-24).

Unbelief

The first sin I'll mention is unbelief. If you don't believe that God will speak to you, then how will you be able to hear His voice? You will dismiss every thought that comes into your head and rational-ize any word you do hear by saying, "That's just me." It's not easy having a relationship with someone who doesn't listen, right? And if you aren't listening because you don't believe you can hear, how can you and God communicate? You must trust that He will speak and that you can hear.

And this goes beyond just hearing God's voice. In Matthew 4:23, it says that Jesus healed "every kind of disease and every kind of sickness among the people." Every disease and sickness. Nothing was too big or small or gross or confusing for Jesus to heal. Your first response may be, "Yeah, but that's, like, Jesus. He's God. He can do anything." Just a few chapters later, however, in Matthew 13:58, while Jesus was in His hometown, ". . . He did not do many miracles there because of their unbelief." It seems that even God can hardly move where there is no trust in Him, but it's more like God offers His help and people say no out of distrust. The people didn't believe Jesus had the authority to heal, so their unbelief got in the way.

Few things bother me more than the phrase, "I guess I just don't have enough faith," or the more sinister, "you didn't have enough faith." As if faith were something that you could measure.

Please.

You either trust God in the situation or you don't. And yes, some people have a more developed trust in God, but only because that's where they are in their relationship with Him. There isn't some sort of holy hierarchy here. Go back to Matthew 13:31-32, a few verses earlier than that "lack of faith" part. Jesus says, "The kingdom of heaven is like a mustard seed, which a man took and sowed in his field; and this is smaller than all other seeds, but when it is full grown, it is larger than the garden plants and becomes a tree, so that THE BIRDS OF THE AIR come and NEST IN ITS BRANCHES."

Just four chapters later, in Matthew 17:19-20, Jesus brings back the image of the mustard seed with His disciples. They had tried to drive a demon out of a boy, and their commands would not work. Jesus had to free the boy from possession. "Then the disciples came to Jesus privately and said, 'Why could we not drive it out?' And He said to them, 'Because of the littleness of your faith; for truly I say to you, if you have faith the size of a mustard seed, you will say to this mountain, "Move from here to there," and it will move; and nothing will be impossible to you.'"

This makes me wonder. Jesus had just told His disciples that they only needed a tiny bit of faith to move mountains, but then told them that they had so little faith. The Bible doesn't explain exactly what Jesus meant by this, but I think the disciples had developed a habit of saying the right words. They had learned how to behave like Jesus, but they had forgotten that the power and authority came through trust in God's power and authority. And then Jesus reminds the disciples if they have faith as small as a mustard seed, "Nothing will be impossible to you."

I remember learning a lesson about the mustard seed in Sunday school. The teachers were trying to empower the kids by telling them that small seeds grow into big trees, and we didn't need to worry if we couldn't do the things that our moms, dads, or pastors did. Our small seeds of faith would eventually grow into big trees of faith. We would eventually arrive.

I have trouble with that view. Jesus told His disciples that they only needed to have the mustard seed sized faith to perform great things. They only needed that little bit of trust. They didn't need to wait for some high degree of faith before they could have that kind of relationship with God. Mustard seeds are pretty small, if you haven't seen one. And that's all it takes to move mountains. So when I hear "I just don't have enough faith," I get a little angry. If you have faith enough to try, and are willing to listen and obey, you will hear God. If you have faith enough to speak the truth, even in uncomfortable situations, truth will overcome the lie.

Confusion sometimes comes because we don't understand the difference between belief and faith. Belief is when a person has mentally accepted and ascribed himself or herself to the truth of the Bible. Faith is when a person acts upon the truth he or she claims to accept.

Now think about this. If we believe what God says, place our trust in Him, and claim that His Word is true, then anything that does not agree with His Word is a lie. That is, whatever contradicts His Word conflicts with the truth, and we should not believe it. For example, the Word says in Isaiah 30:21: "Your ears will hear a word behind you, 'This is the way, walk in it,' whenever you turn to the right or to the left." Exodus 15:26 says that God's people are instructed to listen to His voice. Psalm 95:7-8 calls for an open heart when one hears God's voice. When I read these verses, then I believe that God speaks. It's based on the truth of the Bible. When I start to think that God doesn't ever speak to me, then I have accepted a lie and am unable to hear Him.

Okay, now, if a friend asks me about the weather, and I tell him that it's snowing outside when it's sunny and warm, I've told my friend a lie. What I say does not change the weather, but if my friend has faith in me and dresses in thermals and wool, he will be very uncomfortable. The lie only has power if my friend believes it and acts accordingly.

This brings me to the point of trust and unbelief. Sometimes we see circumstances that seem impossible, or symptoms that appear hopeless. "But I have an inoperable brain tumor, that's there, that's a fact!" "If I don't get that promotion, I won't have the money to pay my bills. That's just the way it is." What are you going to put your trust in more, the "facts" (circumstances and symptoms) or the truth? Jesus told us not to worry about what we will eat or wear, but know that God will feed us and clothe us. We work, but we should not work in anxiety.

Every disease and sickness comes from sin and the curse from Genesis 3, and yet Christ set us free from the bondage of sin and death. Which do we accept? To which kingdom do we surrender, the kingdom of sin, death, and the curse? Or do we surrender to the kingdom of God? If we accept the lie, and do not trust God, then we live our lives in fear because there is no assurance. There is nothing to trust, and we worry. We give the lie power when we accept it, and by accepting the lie, we reject God's Word. And if we have rejected God's Word, then how can we hear His voice? We just told Him to silence it.

Fear

I went through a period where my lack of trust came from unbelief. I called it "The Great Silence." Between the ages of seventeen and nineteen, I seldom heard the voice of God. And even if I did hear Him, I dismissed it or took the advice of my parents as the voice of God. But I didn't want to dismiss God altogether, so I made up reasons as to why I used to hear His voice, but then did no longer. I told people that I was "in the desert, like the Israelites. It was just a time of going without before entering the Promised Land."

But even in the desert, God wanted His people to hear Him. It's just that they were afraid to hear what He had to say. In Exodus 20:18-19 after God speaks the Ten Commandments, "All the people perceived the thunder and the lightning flashes and the sound of the trumpet and the mountain smoking; and when the people saw it, they trembled and stood at a distance. Then they said to Moses, 'Speak to us yourself and we will listen; but let not God speak to us, or we will die.'"

Like I said, I didn't hear God again until I was nineteen years old. I was sitting in my dorm room one night in college reading a Bible. Something within the verses rattled me. The darkness in the room seemed darker. The Christmas lights on my ceiling sharpened and the light became piercing. I knew that the presence of God had entered. I began to repent of lies that I had accepted and even built around me. When I had finished praying, God spoke to me with such power that I felt something I can only describe as a heavy heart. I took off my shoes. After He forgave me, He showed me my identity in Christ and my purpose in life.

Had God stopped speaking to me? No, but I was afraid of what He had to say. I realized that I had made an idol of myself. I wanted to do things my way. I was afraid of what I might have to sacrifice if I followed God's call. What if He wanted me to quit playing music? Or quit writing? I knew that God wanted me to serve Him completely, but I didn't know if I wanted to take on the responsibility if it meant changing my whole life.

One can describe fear as an emotion, something that rises in us when we feel threatened or unable to control a situation. It's a result of feeling unsafe or feeling that others are unsafe. This emotional reaction does exist, and God created our adrenal gland for a reason. But as a believer, I also know that there is a spirit of fear. We can take on that spirit, being fearful always about something. This kind of fear is a lie, a lack of trust in God's sovereignty and protection. People often quote 2 Timothy 1:7 from the King James Version regarding fear, "For God has not given us a spirit of fear, but of power and of love and of a sound mind." When we take on the spirit of fear and do not trust God with the situation, then we have accepted a lie and have sinned.

Fear is a big impediment because of the trust issue. If we trust what God says, the promises He gives us in His Word, then we should have nothing to fear. And I know that it's not always easy to trust a God who is immaterial. It would be nice to have a physical pat on the back from the Most High every time we are faced with a problem. But if we don't trust God because we are afraid, then how can we go to Him for guidance or peace? Haven't we already given power to the lies of fear by believing that God isn't in control of the situation?

Fear can come into our lives in ways so subtle and gradual that we don't even know when we have accepted it into our lives. A few years ago, I had a conversation with my friend Danny at the café where I worked. I hadn't seen him in a while and wanted to know what he had been up to. I said he looked tired. "Yeah, I've been working really hard at school. I haven't been sleeping much."

"Do you have a lot of papers and tests coming up?"

"Not really, I just feel like I have to excel with my work or else it's a waste." I had no real reason to argue with this, so I didn't reply. After a moment he admitted, "Actually, I feel like I have to do well for my parents. They're expecting a lot out of me, and I don't want to let them down."

"Do your parents push you a lot in your achievements, or something?"

"No. I just feel like I have to make them proud."

"Have they ever expressed displeasure in what you've done?"

"Not really, no."

This guy was *afraid*. At some point, he thought that his parents would be disappointed in him if he didn't do everything right the first time. Even though he himself said that they never disapproved of his grades, Danny was convinced that they would criticize him. I told him that he should talk with his parents about it and see what they have to say. If they really did have a condemning attitude about his work, then he should try to have an understanding with them. If they let him know that they loved and supported him without basing their approval on grades, then what did he have to fear?

Danny had to reevaluate his motives because they were sucking the life out of him. Fear was taking all of his strength. He even said that good grades gave him no satisfaction. All of this sounded like bondage to me. Even when Danny prayed to God about something other than his parents or his grades, he still had fear in his life. He wasn't free to have a healthy relationship with God because he was obsessed with reaching goals that were empty to him. His grades and his parents became idols.

See how deep fear can take you? And in ways that seem relatively harmless?

For years, I suffered terrible rejection from my peers. Over time, I developed a deep need to prove myself to them, to gain their favor and avoid their scorn. I put more trust in the validity of what other people thought than the identity that God gave me. I used to look into the mirror and feel grinding in my chest, going over the list of flaws that I saw. "My hair sucks. People stare at my acne. Why is my nose so big? I hate being so skinny." You know the drill.

And it affected my behavior. I would joke about anything and everything to show kids how funny I was so they wouldn't focus on my awkward appearance. I picked on a kid named Matt mercilessly in eighth grade because I thought he was an easy mark. He wore the same clothes two or three days in a row (as I write this, I realize that I haven't changed in two or three days myself), he liked role-playing games like Final Fantasy (which now, as an adult, I have played), and he didn't listen to music (much less rock and roll). I may have scored points with some of the popular kids by showing them newer and hipper ways to make fun of a guy who was already pretty down, but it gave me no real happiness.

I met a girl at church a few years ago. A mutual friend introduced us. After a few minutes, a curious look came to her face. "Wait, are you Isaiah *Kallman?*"

"Yeah, that's me." I thought maybe she had heard of my music.

She narrowed her eyes. "Do you remember Matt from Trinity?"

I told her that I did remember him.

"I'm his sister. You know he left that school because of you."

Oh man, what a heavy thing to hear. After years of rejection and abuse in grade school, I turned it around on another kid to gain credibility with the popular crowd. I asked her to tell Matt that I was sorry. She sneered at me and said, "Tell him yourself," then walked away.

Believe me, if I knew where to find him now, I would.

Basically, this was a "Fear of Man." I trusted in the opinion of others more than God. And instead of glorifying Him by protecting the oppressed and despised, I brought death to someone who was already hurt. I realized how deep my fear of man went when I understood that it influenced my behavior, my self-perception, and my faith ("God, I trust You, except when You tell me that I am wonderfully made and beautiful. And except when You tell me that I'm important and loved" See what I mean?).

Self Hatred

This situation got down into self hate. The fear of my peers' opinion drove me to hate myself and hate others. When asked "Teacher, which is the greatest commandment in the law?" in Matthew 22:36-37, "Jesus replied: 'Love the Lord your God with all your heart and with all your soul and with all your mind.' This is the first and greatest commandment. And the second is like it: 'Love your neighbor as yourself'" (NIV). The whole of the Bible, according to Jesus, rested on the command in Deuteronomy to "Love God, and love others."

If I don't love myself, how can I love my neighbor? I obviously didn't love others if I took cheap shots at kids to get some thin approval. And if I don't love myself, created in the image of God, how can I love God?

When the Holy Spirit revealed this to me and I repented, I have never experienced such freedom. And afterwards, I heard the voice of God again with clarity.

Bitterness and Unforgiveness

Two impediments which often combine themselves to muffle God's voice are bitterness and unforgiveness. A man in our church (we'll call him Hank) had been sent home to die. He had cancer all throughout his body, into his spine, lungs, etc. The doctors had given him about a month to live. A woman in our church saw this man sitting in a chair before a service one Sunday. He looked miserable. She took him over to our church's prayer room, and he grudgingly sat off to the side while a group of people prayed before the service.

During a time of asking God how to pray for Hank, our friend Joseph said that the Lord had given him two words, "bitterness" and "unforgiveness."

Hank's head jerked upright. Everyone noticed. Dad said, "Do those words mean something to you?"

"Yeah."

"Are there some people that you're bitter toward?"

"Yeah."

"Can't forgive them?"

"No."

"Well, Hank, it's killing you."

After a long pause, Hank decided to repent of bitterness and unforgiveness, and then Dad prayed that God would heal and restore Hank's body. Later that week, he felt so healthy and energetic that he scheduled an appointment with his doctor for some testing. The blood work showed no signs of cancer, and a CAT scan confirmed that there was no longer any cancer in his body. His doctor said, "You're not going to believe this, but you don't have cancer anymore. You can go home."

I really wish the story ended there. For well over a year, we gave Hank's testimony with much joy and praised God. The thing is, Hank took on those feelings of bitterness and unforgiveness again. The cancer came back and grew wildly. He died two years later. While no one except God can say for sure, I believe he died because he again agreed with those old feelings of bitterness and unforgiveness. He took the sin and illness back into his life.

I imagine God pleading with people like Hank, crying out for restoration when that person's back is turned in stubbornness. I can picture this having happened:

"Please forgive the person whom you are hating. It is killing you, not them."

"Well, I don't want to die, so I'll repent and turn my face back to you."

But when there is no restoration of the relationship between the man and the person whom he could not forgive, that spirit of bitterness came back and found "the house swept clean." The man maybe built more bitterness toward the other person because that person had not suffered as he had suffered with his illness. "He's the one in the wrong! Why did I almost die for something *he* did? It's not fair!" (It brings to mind the old saying, "you can't drink poison and expect the other person to die.") Then the state of that man is worse off than before, and he has rejected God's mercy, allowing sin to come between them.

Anger

These sins stem from and feed into another impediment, anger. Going back to "The Greatest Command" in Deuteronomy to love God and love others, we are called to hate only that which God hates. This is commonly called "righteous anger," and it does serve a good purpose that glorifies God. But when someone does something that makes us angry, robbery for example, and we begin to hate the person who committed the act, taking our focus off of the sin of theft and wishing harm on the thief, we hate our neighbor, a person bearing the image and breath of God.

When the Pharisees and Torah instructors brought an adulterous woman to Jesus in John 8, they asked Jesus if they should stone her. This is that lovely story where Jesus responds, "He who is without sin among you, let him be the first to throw a stone at her" (v. 7). One by one, the older ones first, the men from the mob drop their stones and leave. Here's the part that I want you to notice. Jesus looks up from drawing a picture (or something, it's never clear what He scratched out in the dust) and says to the woman, "'Woman, where are they? Did no one condemn you?' She said, 'No one, Lord.' And Jesus said, 'I do not condemn you, either. Go. From now on sin no more'" (vv. 10-11).

Jesus understood that everyone sins, and if we identify people with their sins (e.g., a thief steals and an adulterer cheats), then we are doomed. There's no redemption in the life of a man who once told a lie and is known as a liar the rest of his life, even if he has repented and changed his ways.

Anger can blind this perspective, and we can impose the sin upon the person, making the sin and the person one and the same. When a person becomes consumed with anger, it leads to bitterness, a long-standing grudge birthed out of anger. If that person holds on to the grudge, they are unable to forgive until they give up the sin and repent. Anger. Bitterness. Unforgiveness.

I keep using that word, repent, and I sometimes wonder if I sound like one of those street-side evangelists peddling guilt by pointing out all the sin that keeps people in bondage. I don't want to be a bummer and leave you without any hope. The reason we must understand the sin which gets in the way of our hearing God is that He wants us to communicate with Him, to have an open relationship with Him. If we're holding on to any sin, if we've never addressed it and asked for forgiveness, then we've never accepted the forgiveness. If we want to live in the freedom God offers, we must confess our sins and allow God to change us.

In the story of Jesus and the adulterous woman, we learn that repentance doesn't bring condemnation. Repentance, going back to my picture earlier, means that we've chosen to change our clothes (or costume or uniform, whatever you can identify with) when we realized that it wasn't snowing in August. Surely that frees us more than condemns us.

I don't want you to focus on all of your problems and try to become perfect before seeking a relationship with God. Otherwise, you would never *have* a relationship with God because you would be preoccupied with fixing yourself. And trust me, our restoration is an ongoing process.

But you do not fix yourself. You do not heal yourself. You do not save yourself. The Word says in Titus 3:3-7,

> For we also once were foolish ourselves, disobedient, deceived, enslaved to various lusts and pleasures, spending our life in malice and envy, hateful, hating one another. But when the kindness of God our Savior and His love for mankind appeared, He saved us, not on the basis of deeds which we have done in righteousness, but according to His mercy, by the washing of regeneration and renewing by the Holy Spirit, whom He poured out upon us richly through Jesus Christ our Savior, so that being justified by His grace we would be made heirs according to the hope of eternal life.

The point is spiritual growth. Healing. Freedom. Redemption. Deepening our relationship with the God of the Universe. I believe repentance allows us to come closer to God, and allows Him to come closer to us. I believe it brings balance to our lives.

CHAPTER 4

Circles, Triangles, and Balloons

Understanding the Balance of the Physical and Spiritual

"And Jesus kept increasing in wisdom and stature, and in favor with God and men." (Lk. 2:52)

"Therefore I urge you, brethren, by the mercies of God, to present your bodies a living and holy sacrifice, acceptable to God, which is your spiritual service of worship. And do not be conformed to this world, but be transformed by the renewing of your mind, so that you may prove what the will of God is, that which is good and acceptable and perfect." (Rom. 12:1-2)

hen my parents attended Spring Arbor College, they used to attend meetings on campus called "Body Life." These meetings were led by Bob and Ray Husband and Steve Anzur, who all worked for the school. Mom and Dad often talk about how these men fed into their spiritual lives.

At one of the Body Life meetings, Bob (or Ray, they were twins, and my parents have a hard time remembering who said what) taught on Luke 2:52 and living a balanced life modeled after Jesus. "And

Jesus kept increasing in wisdom and stature, and in favor with God and men." They drew a triangle and a circle on a chalkboard to represent the verse visually.

Then they labeled the sides of the triangle with the words "Wisdom," "Stature," and "Favor with Man," placing "Favor with God" in the circle.

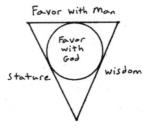

The gist of the teaching out of Luke was that every part of our lives fit into the three areas of the triangle: the physical, mental, and relational. The circle represents our spirit, our relationship with God, and this is connected to every other part of our lives. It was the same for Jesus.

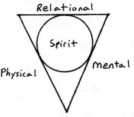

In other words, you cannot separate your spiritual life from who you are physically, mentally, or relationally. It all weaves together and needs balance, lined up with God by His Spirit.

I first heard Dad teach this concept in our basement on a big whiteboard when I was fifteen years old. Over the years the Circle/Triangle has morphed into an in-depth teaching on health, balance, and organizational structure called the Unified Vision Framework.

But what do circles and triangles have to do with hearing God?

God is deeply creative and will use everything at His disposal to communicate and grow closer to His children. When we listen, God will use thoughts, physical events, and social relationships to speak to us and to confirm His voice.

We covered how God can speak to us in our thoughts in the chapter about listening. He may give us a thought, a song, or a mental picture. He may give us a dream. When writing to churches in the ancient Greek city of Corinth, Paul set about explaining different spiritual gifts given to believers. "But to each one is given the manifestation of the Spirit for the common good. For to one is given the word of wisdom through the Spirit, and to another the word of knowledge according to the same Spirit" (1 Cor. 12:7-8). And then the list goes on. My point here is that God speaks to us mentally.

God often uses the Scriptures to speak to us. While you might think that this is obvious, I would like to add a twist. As you read the Bible, ask God to communicate with you through words. When you come to a verse or a word or thought that strikes you, stop. Ask God what this verse means to you, for the *rhema* word. Why did that thought rise up? Meditate on the verse. Think about the context. Learn about the people that the writer addressed. Look up the words in a concordance and look at the cross-references. In Ezekiel 3:1 God told the prophet to eat the scrolls. When you "eat" the scroll, you take it in, immerse yourself in it, researching the context and let it become a part of your life. Expect that God has something specific for you in those words. I have spent months in one verse and God has revealed things about my heart and life that I never would have understood without paying attention to the little nudge in my spirit.

For example, I read Matthew 9 and had to stop at verses 14 through 17. It was as if the Holy Spirit put those verses into bold print. In that chapter, Jesus had just called Matthew to follow Him and afterwards went to a party. While He partied down with everyone, some people began to ask Him questions.

> Then the disciples of John came to Him, asking, "Why do we and the Pharisees fast, but Your disciples do not fast?"
>
> And Jesus said to them, "The attendants of the bridegroom cannot mourn as long as the bridegroom is with them, can they? But the days will come when the bridegroom is taken away from them, and then they will fast." (Mt. 9:14-15)

Okay, no problem there. I figured Jesus meant that people should rejoice when the Son of God is with them. The day would come when He would leave, and then the disciples would have reason to fast. But Jesus didn't stop there, and I didn't understand why He said this next:

> But no one puts a patch of unshrunk cloth on an old garment; for the patch pulls away from the garment,

and a worse tear results. Nor do people put new wine into old wineskins; otherwise the wineskins burst, and the wine pours out and the wineskins are ruined; but they put new wine into fresh wineskins, and both are preserved. (Mt. 9:16-17)

Why did Jesus tack on that bit about sewing and wineskins? What did that have to do with fasting?

I prayed about that verse for two years. Not exclusively, mind you. There were other issues that needed prayer and God taught me many other things in that time. But every now and again, those verses would come to mind and I asked God to give me under-standing. One day, He gave me understanding. The Pharisees and John's disciples were living according to age-old traditions and their inherited interpretations of scripture. Jesus did not tell them to stop fasting. He was saying that there is a time for a parties and a time for fasting.

Besides that, Jesus wanted to remind them that even though God sometimes commands a fast, God also commands His people to celebrate. Although He didn't claim that their understanding of fasting was wrong or out-of-date, there was a certain way to patch old clothes and store new wine. It really was an emphasis of "a time and place for everything" (for example, read Deuteronomy 16:1-16 where God explains how and when the Hebrew people, former Egyptian slaves, should have a party).

The formal process used by some churches to facilitate this com-munication with God by using the Scriptures is called *Lectio Divina* where one sits quietly, reads a passage out loud and then meditates on it. But you don't necessarily need a formal process to have God speak to you through the Word. Just be patient, expect that He will speak, and pay attention.

He also speaks to us relationally. There are several stories from people who prayed seeking wisdom from God, and then received a phone call from a friend who at that moment just thought of something to tell them. When God sent me on that March road trip, he had me stay in a house in Nashville. The girls living there asked me why I had gone on this journey, and I told them about obedience to God through listening. One of the girls said, "You needed to come here. I've been asking God for direction in my life, but I didn't know how to find it." I stayed up most of the night talking to her and her roommates, explaining how they could hear God's voice.

The nudge might come from the physical realm. I have a friend who stops to pray and receives a hug from God every time she sees two geese flying together. It is a code from the Father saying that He loves her and watches over her.

It can also come from within your physical body. I'll sometimes refer to my "spidey-sense" (as in the "Amazing Spider-Man" comic books) when I feel a move in the spirit. That is, I get a tingle at a certain point in my neck and at the back of my head. And as silly as the spidey-sense sounds, it has caused me to act and pray in situations that were pretty serious. Situations that I wouldn't have recognized without that direction from the Spirit.

During a Wednesday night gathering at my church, a guy came in and sat down near the back row. I was leading worship, and only glanced at him. My head began to feel those pinpricks and I asked God what was going on. The Holy Spirit led me to silence any menacing spirits and command them to leave. I turned away from the microphone for a moment and whispered my prayer toward the wall.

So, I know that nobody heard or saw me say it. I know that doesn't sound very bold and authoritative, but the guy got up and left the room. After a few minutes, he walked through the door and stopped short. He looked around confused, muttered, and walked out for good. As it turns out, this guy would come in and say all sorts of strange and upsetting things to people during worship or prayer, and God used the spidey-sense to direct my prayer for protection.

Dad also has nudges from the Holy Spirit in his physical body. This happened one time while he taught at a church in Jenison, Michigan. He had everyone take a minute to be quiet and let God speak. He sat down on the front row and got quiet himself. As he listened, he felt a sharp pain in his abdomen. So he asked the Lord, "What was that?" The thought immediately came into his head "There is a person here with a liver problem. I want you to pray for her healing." Dad started to argue with God. He really did not want to say anything about what he had just heard. A wall of discomfort rose up with full force in his heart and mind.

What would you do? He had never done or said anything remotely like this in any of his teaching, but he knew it was God. He informed the Lord that this was a Reformed church and that they would not be comfortable. God did not seem bothered by this fact at all. Then Dad told the Lord the odds of a person having a liver problem in a crowd of four hundred people (slim to none) and again God did not seem distressed. As everyone quietly sat and prayed, Dad sat in the front row wrestling with God, sweating and looking for an exit.

So what did the bold man of faith and power do? Couch it and make it sound like a normal, everyday thing. He said, "As we were quiet I had a sharp pain in my liver. I believe that there might be someone here with a liver problem and I will be staying after the service to pray for people. So if there is someone here with a liver problem, please come and see me afterwards. I believe the Lord wants to heal you. As a matter of fact, if anyone would like prayer after the service, come down and I will pray for you" He used as many qualifying words as he could. At least someone might come down for prayer so he would not look completely foolish. "So much for boldly stepping out in faith," he later told me.

Dad prayed for people after the service and many amazing things happened that night. At the very end of the line, a woman said, "I am the liver." She had suffered from liver cancer years before and had gone into remission, but the previous week some tests showed that it was coming back and she was gripped by fear. Dad explained that God wanted her to know that He understood her suffering and He was going to do something for her. Dad prayed for God to act according to His word and she felt a great peace. We later learned that she went back for more tests and the cancer had disappeared.

God spoke to Dad through a physical pain. He asked, listened, obeyed, and God responded with a supernatural result. God will use thoughts, physical events, and other people to communicate with us and confirm His voice. We have to pay attention, but He speaks to us and confirms what He says all the time.

It is generally believed in Christianity that when a person accepts Jesus as his Savior, when he puts his trust in Christ, then God's Spirit will reside in him. This is taken from Galatians 2:20, "I have been crucified with Christ; and it is no longer I who live, but Christ lives in me; and the life which I now live in the flesh I live by faith in the Son of God, who loved me and gave Himself up for me."

The deeper our relationship grows with God, where we learn how to obey the desires of His heart, the more people see Christ in us. For example, how we respond to people who are being rude will reflect either our nature or Christ's. I don't know about you, but I have actually met and interacted with people who are mean or rude or caustic or all of the above at the same time. Since I have the Holy Spirit in me, I can hear in my mind and heart how to respond when someone treats me, or another person, poorly. When they see me respond with kindness or in peace or in love, they are drawn to Christ. It's not me, but Christ *in me* that responds with love. Let's look at our diagram again. This time the circle is larger and covers part of the triangle.

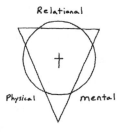

I want to illustrate by this last picture that, as we respond in faith to God's direction and obey His leading, our actions and words begin to become true reflections of God's heart. When people see our actions or hear our words, they see and hear God. John the Baptist said it this way: "He must increase, but I must decrease" (Jn. 3:30). I have found that listening helps this process. When I stop focusing on myself, God is able to speak and move in my life, and my spiritual person influences my outside person with each step. Think about points of conflict when someone is rude and we respond in love. Think about when we dismiss unkind or lustful thoughts from our minds rather than dwelling on them. When the world sees this in my behavior, it begins to see less of me and more of Christ. The inner circle expands and people are drawn to the Spirit of God in us by what they observe.

This next diagram shows the second aspect of our life with God. We are in Christ.

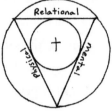

When we turn over everything that we are to God and accept Jesus as God's Son, we are spiritually placed "In Christ." Our triangle, everything that we are as a created being, is now viewed by God through Jesus. That is, when God looks at us, He doesn't see who we used to be as sinners. He sees His redeemed children, hidden in the work and person of Jesus (Col. 3:3). The walk of a Christian, then, is to get our inner circle to resemble the outer circle of who we are "In Christ" and bring the two closer together. The path that accelerated and changed my growth toward this resemblance has been listening to God's voice. When I don't know how to act or respond to a situation, God instructs me and I do my best to obey. Hearing and obeying God had a transforming effect in my life that was not present when my prayers were spiritual voice mail.

Now let's take it even further. Think of your spirit as a balloon and replace the Circle-within-the-Triangle with this balloon.

In Romans 12:2, the writer exhorts us to avoid conforming to this world but rather be transformed by the renewing of our minds.

A balloon helps me understand this verse. When Dad teaches this, he draws a finger pressing on the balloon, causing the shape to change.

It makes an indentation on the balloon with a "conforming pressure." The finger intentionally changes the shape of the balloon and makes it look different than its natural state. Now, take a minute and think about some conforming pressures in your life.

A conforming pressure can be a thought, action, or word spoken that draws us away from God and how He created us to live. This might surprise you, but the truth is that all men struggle with lust. An old axiom says that 97 percent of all men admit to struggling with lust, the other 3 percent are lying. What is that? It's a conforming pressure that the enemy uses to try and destroy us. Although the attacks come in many ways and through many senses, the enemy ultimately wants to warp our thoughts and control us.

Another conforming pressure is fear. We see this every week in a Wednesday night gathering we lead called the "W." (Worship, wrestling, warfare, wholeness, Wednesday, whatever . . . we couldn't decide so we just call it "W.") We pray with people nearly every week who are wracked with fear, and their fear has an enormously negative impact on their bodies and relationships. Fear is a pressure that tries to make you lose trust in God and focus on the broken world we live in.

I could go on about the various conforming pressures and their negative impact on people's lives. Suffice to say there are a whole lot of people walking around with spirit balloons indented like golf balls. They are being conformed and many of them do not even realize it.

So what do we do about it? According to Romans 12:2, we allow God to renew our minds and transform us. When my parents first told me this, I said, "Fine, thanks for the help." As you can see, one point of pressure in my own life was cynicism. I had trouble knowing how to practically apply the verse to my life. But when I stop to think about it, what is the only thing that can keep the shape of the balloon from changing when pressure is exerted on its surface?

Transforming pressure is the only thing that will allow the balloon to maintain its shape with an equal or greater pressure from inside the balloon. For every action, there needs to be an equal and opposite reaction, right? This scientific concept reflects the truth of the verse, "greater is He who is in you than he who is in the world" (1 Jn. 4:4). Strong, transforming, internal pressure that helps us take thoughts captive and choose to do what is right even in difficult circumstances.

I have found that as I pay attention to God, the lies and pressures of life begin to weaken. He speaks the truth to me, and the truth sets me free. It smoothes out my balloon. It puts my life in balance. When there is less of me and more of Him, the impact from all the conforming pressures that try to destroy me every day diminishes. I have a greater pressure inside that counters all of the conforming pressures from outside.

When I understood how God brings balance into my life, I felt great relief. I didn't have to struggle in agony over those conforming pressures because I could rely on God to smooth them out. But how? Just by asking? Is it really that easy? Well, maybe not as easy as we'd like. It is simple, but not easy. The balanced life (circle/triangle and smooth balloon) doesn't necessarily come with the snap of your fingers. It comes with the relationship that you build with God. You learn how to listen, how to give more of your life to Him, how to trust Him despite the circumstances. It comes with intimacy.

CHAPTER 5

Intimacy
The Point

"An emphasis on spiritual technique may well lead us away from the passionate relationship that God values above all. More than a doctrinal system, more than a mystical experience, the Bible emphasizes a relationship with a Person, and personal relationships are never steady-state."—Philip Yancey [13]

veryone at some point in his or her life looks at prayer liturgically, that is, as a traditional routine in worship. Whether a person believes in God or not, prayer can seem like something that is done out of compulsion, habit, or need. A believer can say he or she talks to God, but in reality just talks at Him. "Help me with this, please fix that, and make that person change." You get the idea.

In the same way, people can look at faith like a ritual. They have been told to "believe" for so long that even if they do profess their faith in God, they couldn't explain to you why. They always have believed and that's why they believe.

Something happened when Adam and Eve first sinned:

Then the eyes of both of them were opened, and they knew that they were naked; and they sewed fig leaves together and made themselves loin coverings. They heard the sound of the LORD God walking in the garden in the cool of the day, and the man and his wife hid themselves from the presence of the LORD God among the trees of the garden." (Gen. 3:7-8)

This leads me to believe that God walked with His creation and spoke with them personally because *they knew* He was walking toward them.

The next verse, Genesis 3:9, says, "Then the LORD God called to the man, and said to him, 'Where are you?'" It's probably safe to say that God knew Adam and Eve were hiding in the trees. He is God, after all. But this question, "Where are you?" indicates that there was a separation between man and God. The intimacy God had with man was lost. Sin caused this separation and then man tried to hide out of fear and shame. Something happened then, and it is still happening today.

It seems like we still hide from God, even in our prayers and in our faith, when He created us to have a relationship with Him. And I mean really walk with Him and talk with Him. We hide by creating religious structures and programs that make us feel safe but have no life. Or praying (stating our need) and going off to do what we planned to do from the start, asking God to bless it. We hide by praying without waiting to hear God's answer, or without believing He will answer at all. That way, if things don't go the way we planned, we have some isolated Bible verses to fall back on, saying God's ways are higher than our ways, or maybe we had too little faith. We hide in a faith best explained by doctrine, dogma, and a shoulder shrug.

It seems that we don't want to endure the hard work and discomfort of a relationship. Why? Because we're afraid of the risk that comes with relationship, and we'd be ashamed if we couldn't explain ourselves. We're afraid of rejection. What happened to the faith that had the beauty and mystery of falling in love?

At the end of Genesis 3, God does a marvelous thing. He kills two animals in order to cover the naked Adam and Eve. Not only does this symbolize the sacrifice needed to atone for their sins, but it shows that God had not abandoned them. He still wanted to be involved in their lives.

In the following books of the Bible, over time, God instructs the people of Israel to build a place for His Presence to reside (Exodus 26). This eventually became the temple in Jerusalem. There was an inner room called the Holy Place where the priests made animal sacrifices for the atonement of sins. And in the Holy Place, there was another room sectioned off by a massive, heavy curtain called the Most Holy Place. This is where the Spirit of God resided. Only the high priest could enter the Most Holy Place, and even then only at certain times. After a ritual cleansing, the high priest performed specific and detailed sacrifices before God (Lev. 16:2-25). These were the rules set up by God so that He could still interact with man when sin separated them.

When Jesus went to the temple in John 2:14-16, "He found in the temple those who were selling oxen and sheep and doves, and the money changers seated at their tables. And He made a scourge of cords, and drove them all out of the temple, with the sheep and the oxen; and He poured out the coins of the money changers and overturned their tables; and to those who were selling the doves He said, 'Take these things away; stop making My Father's house a place of business.'"

The Jews were angry with Jesus and demanded to know what right He had to drive anyone out of the temple. In John 2:19-21, "Jesus answered them, 'Destroy this temple, and in three days I will raise it up.' The Jews then said, 'It took forty-six years to build this temple, and will You raise it up in three days?' But He was speaking of the temple of His body."

The central teaching of the Christian church is that God came to earth as a man, Jesus, lived a sinless life, died on a cross, and then rose from the dead. His death represented the final sacrifice for the sin of mankind, as prophesied in Isaiah 53. But because Jesus got up from the grave and is the sacrifice that still lives, God no longer requires animal sacrifice for atonement.

Also, in Matthew 27:51, when Jesus died, the temple curtain tore from top to bottom. The separation caused by sin had been broken, and God began to reconcile Himself with man. No more high priest as intermediary, no more ritual cleansing. Man could again interact with God and not fear death.

Now I know that we can trust what God says in Jeremiah 29:12-13: "Then you will call upon Me and come and pray to Me, and I will listen to you. You will seek Me and find Me when you search for Me with all your heart." The Word says here that if we seek Him we will find Him, but how exactly can we "seek God"? And when we find Him, then what?

Dad led worship for ten years in a church. Soon after he began, he noticed certain cues our pastor would give him. Whether the pastor wanted Dad to cut things short or keep worshipping, all he had to do was look at my dad a certain way. At the end of his sermons, he had a different cadence to his voice that let Dad know he should get up on stage and start playing softly behind him before closing with a time of worship. Even though they didn't necessarily set up this code over lunch somewhere, Dad just knew what he was trying to communicate.

My parents have a similar unspoken code between them. Sometimes, Dad can tell when Mom is tired and needs a cup of coffee, or when she wants to talk before they go to bed. She won't always say, but he knows by the look on her face, or just feels a vibe in the room. Of course other times, she'll poke his leg or nudge his foot when he's not paying attention to her clues. Let's be honest, though. Sometimes we all need a stronger hint.

He told me that he didn't recognize these signals right away when he met my mother or ministered with our old pastor. He learned how to understand them better the more he got to know the person. By building a relationship with them, he gained an intimacy that allowed him to know and trust them, and they him.

In the Psalms, God tells His people, "I will instruct you and teach you in the way which you should go; I will counsel you with My eye upon you" (Psalm 32:8). Like any other relationship, we have to work to reach this level of intimate communication. Spend time with God, get to know Him better. Before reading the Word, ask God to open your heart to its teaching and make it come alive. When you pray, listen for the little thought. Find a quiet place where no one will interrupt you as you learn more about God. Let the *rhema* breathe into your spirit and guide you into truth.

Caught Up in Religion

When I talk with people about intimacy with God, they'll sometimes get caught up in a talk about religion. I think that we often misuse the word "religion." This is important, so read this carefully. Religion is the devotion one shows to the thing in which they believe. I want to make sure we understand that *faith* is the result of our intimacy with God, the trust we have built in Him. On the other hand, *religion* is merely the framework in which that relationship lives.

When Dad and I first talked about this, and he said the word "framework," I told him it sounded like management-speak. Frameworks and paradigms and stuff. But then he came up with a pretty good picture. My parents, brothers, sister, we're a family. We have rules set so we can understand how to best live with each other. The gathering of those who have accepted Christ as their Savior and are trying to follow Him, that is the church. But the Church typically meets in a building. They have a "declaration of faith." A doctrine. Certain accepted interpretations of the Scripture. An order to their worship and teaching. It's a structure added onto their faith. That is the religious framework surrounding their faith, but all of those things are not their *faith*.

Even this isn't a complete description of the difference between religion and relationship. My father loves my mother. Sometimes, ten minutes before dinner, Mom will notice that something is missing and ask Dad to go to the grocery store for, like, a loaf of bread. And he'll go, even though he's hungry and tired, even though it seems inconvenient. It's a simple picture, but I think you get the idea. My father serves my mother because he loves her, but his service is not his love. When a person begins to think that service is love—that tasks are love—then it becomes nothing more than duty. It's easy for us to become so driven to do God's work that we neglect God.

Focus on knowing God first, talking with Him and understanding His heart. When you have that relationship with Him, though, He'll direct your steps. He'll ask you to get a loaf of bread ten minutes before dinner or to go stand on your head at the 7-Eleven.

This sets the foundation for so much in your life as a believer, for building a real relationship with the God of the universe. The better we discern His voice, the easier it is to trust Him. When He tells us to do something, we know to obey even when it looks stupid. Why? Because the more we know Him, the easier it is to love Him, and Love can make a person do some crazy things.

CHAPTER 6

Stark Raving Obedience

Learning to Trust God

My family has heard about and seen some pretty amazing miracles that happened after people obeyed God's voice. The willingness of people to follow through on the direction of the Holy Spirit allowed God to work in their lives or in the lives of others in profound ways.

In one instance, God told a young woman, "Give the Kallmans bags of frozen chicken." Back then, my family didn't have much money, and we had very little food. I remembered feeling frustrated. My family had tried to follow what we heard from God. *Why wasn't He blessing us?* we wondered. That night, my family had just sat down to a humble dinner of seasoned rice (I was at band practice raiding someone else's fridge at the time) when they heard this woman knock at the door. According to Dad, no one in our family had ever met her before, and to this day he's not sure if she even introduced herself. She handed the food to my dad and said that she had been told in a dream to give us food. Although she knew that our family lived in the general area, she had no idea which road we lived on, much less in which house. She had gone from door to door asking people if they knew where she could find the Kallmans. Someone eventually told her where to find us. My family praised God for His provision and thanked the woman before she left. I am almost sure she had a moment or two during her search for our house where she questioned whether she had really heard God's direction.

Crazy? Absolutely, but it was part of God's provision for my family. I know *I'm* glad that the woman listened and pushed through her own discomfort to obey God. Now she has more reason to trust in the voice of the Holy Spirit and have confidence in God's provision for her life because she saw the result of her obedience. Everyone is blessed, everyone is encouraged, and everyone is built up in their faith. And we ate chicken for a month.

Even though I love this story, I need to remind you that prayer should not be an activity in which we engage in order to get something from God. Or, as Ray C. Stedman said, "True prayer is never a man's plans which he brings to God for Him to bless."[14] Prayer should be the activity that allows us to be with God and changes us as a result of that intimacy.

Sometimes, prayer sounds like another word for "begging." We'll close our eyes, and try to imagine a God that is right next to us, even if we don't see Him. Then, we go on to say things like, "Oh God, please help me to be happy," or "Lord, I need some money to pay off my debt next Thursday." Sure, we can say these prayers, but it leaves little room for growth or relationship.

Let's say God speaks to someone's heart to give you some money. Maybe He'll open up a good job opportunity in answer to your prayer. Even if you give thanks, what lesson have you learned? For a lot of people, the lesson looks something like this, "If I ask God for something I need, He'll give it to me." At that point, God's relationship with us is about as deep as that of a nice guy who gives some change to a homeless person on the street. And then, we don't come back to God until we need more change.

If that's how we pray, then we are bums. Spiritual bums, but still bums. And are we really better off with another blessed quarter? Are the real deep, heavy needs and desires of our hearts actually satiated by another bottle of cheap spiritual wine?

I do not want anyone reading this to think they have to follow a certain formula to get a guaranteed result. Listening prayer is a way for God to commune with us. I've found that it cultivates a healthy and complete relationship with Him. I am trying to remember as I write this book that, as C. S. Lewis said in *Letters to Malcom*, "the charge to Peter was 'feed my sheep'; not 'try experiments on my rats,' or even 'teach my performing dogs new tricks.'"[15] It is not about what we do or the assignments we fulfill, it is about who we are as His servants, friends, children. It's about the relationship.

Listening + Obedience = Blessing

Listening plus Obedience results in Blessing. I used to think that this was just a reworking of "Name it/Claim it" theology, the kind of thing I sometimes hear about on TV and makes my skin all clammy. The focus of Name it/Claim it is "me" and my wants and desires, whereas the focus of L + O = B is the Father. It is also the biblical pattern for a walk of obedience. L + O = B is something I've observed, a natural result of obedience, but it's not a formula to live by. Believe me, if I wanted to live by formulas, I would have enjoyed algebra and geometry a whole lot more.

Joyce Huggett, in her book *The Joy of Listening to God,* states, "I find it easier to write about obedience, read about obedience, and preach about obedience than to obey. I know how to leap this hurdle: simply discover God's will and do it. But I find it hard."[16] Or as Jonathan Graf, founder of *Pray!* magazine, puts it, "Learning to obey is a difficult process. We want to hear God speak. But then we find ourselves wanting to weigh whether or not we should do what we hear."[17] This is the crux of listening prayer. If we pursue God and His voice to gain direction and guidance and then ignore what He gives, we are at risk. His expectation is that, as servants, or more deeply as friends, we will obey. It is not even a question.

Also, if we choose not to obey, there are consequences. In Luke 6:47-49, Jesus reassures us that obedience is not about avoiding punishment, but having a balanced, stable life.

> Everyone who comes to Me and hears My words and acts on them, I will show you whom he is like: he is like a man building a house, who dug deep and laid a foundation on the rock; and when a flood occurred, the torrent burst against that house and could not shake it, because it had been well built. But the one who has heard and has not acted accordingly, is like a man who built a house on the ground without any foundation; and the torrent burst against it and immediately it collapsed, and the ruin of that house was great.

Hebrews 3:15 says, "Today if you hear His voice, do not harden your hearts, as when they provoked Me." When the people of Israel wandered in the desert, they complained to Moses that God had failed them. They said it would have been better to be slaves in Egypt than to die in the wilderness. Through Moses, God had proved

Himself to Israel several times with food called "manna" appearing miraculously every day, with flocks of quail coming daily for them to eat, with water pouring out of rocks. Still, the Israelites defied God with hardened hearts.

In Deuteronomy 28:15, God gave the people of Israel a warning. "But it shall come about, if you do not obey the LORD your God, to observe to do all His commandments and His statutes with which I charge you today, that all these curses will come upon you and overtake you." Then it goes on to list dozens of curses. I'd like to point out that God does not say that He will curse you, but that the curses will come and overtake you. When we obey God's voice, we allow Him to move in our lives, but if we ignore God, over time we leave ourselves open to misery.

Faking obedience is even worse. According to Psalm 81:15, if we pretend obedience, then we hate God. Not the best way to realize an intimate relationship with God, in my opinion.

We can observe the first instance (or failure) of L + O = B in the scripture with Adam and Eve. God forbade them to eat from the Tree of the Knowledge of Good and Evil. They heard and knew what He required. The serpent made an appeal to Eve's "self." She listened to the lie and chose to disobey. This marked the beginning of man's separation from God and brought death into the world.

My father once heard Charles Stanley say, "All suffering traces back to people hearing God but not obeying." It's easy for me to read this sentence and place the blame of sin and suffering on Adam and Eve. It's their fault, right? Francis Schaeffer gives a more direct statement in his book, *The God Who Is There*: "The heart of the rebellion of Satan and man was the desire to be autonomous."[18] This means that when I want to do things my way, or I'm worried that

God's direction will only bring me sorrow and I act accordingly, I've joined in the rebellion of man against God. The good news here is that even though Adam and Eve were disobedient, God still pursued them. He still wanted a relationship and restoration, and He wants the same for us. We do not have to look too hard to see the truth of this statement throughout the Bible.

Adam and Eve show us the downside of L + O = B. For the positive, turn to Deuteronomy 28:1-2 in the King James Version where it says (emphasis mine), "and it shall come to pass, if thou shalt *hearken diligently unto the voice* of Jehovah thy God, to *observe to do all his commandments* which I command thee this day, that Jehovah thy God will set thee on high above all the nations of the earth: *and all these blessings shall come upon thee*, and overtake thee, if thou shalt hearken unto the voice of Jehovah thy God." It then goes on to list the blessings. I don't know about you, but I want the list of blessings and not the list of curses.

By the way, I love one of the interpretations of the Hebrew in the phrase about blessings. It translates "overtake you" as "chase you down and run you over." In other words, you cannot avoid the blessings. They will chase you down and run you over if you obey. I want that truck to hit me full force.

Consider Jesus' parable of the talents in Matthew 25. The first two servants obeyed the master by investing the money he had given them and making a return. The third servant buried the money his master had given him in the ground. When the master returned, he was overjoyed at the faithfulness of the first two servants and invites them, "enter into the joy of your master." With the third servant, he becomes furious and strips the man of everything he has, throwing him out into a place of anguish.

Why did the master act so harshly? Maybe the servant kept the money for himself hoping that the master wouldn't return. There were robbers that would wait for merchants to pass by on trade routes. The servant also called his master a "hard man, reaping where you did not sow and gathering where you scattered no seed." Maybe he expected his master to anger the people from far away and get himself killed. Who knows?

More importantly, I think we should look at the third servant and wonder, "What was he thinking, burying the talent in the ground?" The master had asked the servant to care for a large sum of money in trust, and the servant did not obey. It would make sense that the servant was afraid of failure, that he would lose his master's money. Maybe he didn't have faith in himself, even though the master had enough faith in him to entrust a great deal of money to his care. He did not serve the master, so he was no longer a servant, and he was thrown out of the master's house. Hearing and obeying allows God's blessing, but disobedience opens us to disaster.

Living Stark Raving Obedience

If you read the Bible, think about some of the things God said to people. He asked them to do some remarkably stupid things by human standards.

- "Build a huge boat in your yard. I know you don't know how to do it, but I'll show you." (Genesis 6)
- "Pick up everything you own and leave town. I will tell you where you're going when you get there." (Genesis 12)
- "Kill your son. Wow, you were really going to do that, huh? Well, don't kill him. I wanted to test your faithfulness." (Genesis 22)

- "Walk up this mountain during an earthquake." (Exodus 19)

And it was not limited to the Old Testament.

Acts 8:26-40 tells the story of the apostle Philip. God told him to walk down the Gaza road into the desert. Do you think Philip had a schedule that day, things to do, people to see, ministry to perform? I'll bet he did. But when the Holy Spirit told him to go, he went. Why? I couldn't tell you. I don't know. The Bible only says that he heard and obeyed.

All right, out on his stroll into the desert, the Holy Spirit directed Philip to stand next to a chariot. Philip heard an Ethiopian eunuch, the Queen's treasurer, reading a passage out of the book of Isaiah in the chariot. The eunuch said, "Who can explain this to me?" And Philip said, "Oh, that would be me." Philip began to tell the man of how this passage spoke of one chosen by God to redeem the world. This promised one, the Messiah, had come, and His name was Jesus. Right then and there, the eunuch accepted Christ and Philip baptized him.

Let's put this story into a modern context. Imagine that you wake up one morning, and you hear the voice of the Holy Spirit tell you to go to stand on a busy street corner in your town. Does that sound like God? It sounds kind of strange, right? Okay, imagine you've obeyed and now the Holy Spirit tells you, "walk up to the stretch limo and knock on the window." Now, does that sound like God? No, it actually sounds *profoundly* stupid, but that's what Philip did. And his obedience still has an effect today.

The queen of Ethiopia became a Christian because of her treasurer's conversion and built a palace in Jerusalem for a future pilgrimage. In 2000, I went with a group of people to help restore the rooms of the servant's quarters of this palace. The building was being converted into apartments for Jewish immigrants coming to Israel through Bridges for Peace, a Christian outreach in Jerusalem. We didn't go to Israel to preach Jesus on the street corners (it's against the law to proselytize there), but we did show God's love for His chosen people by serving them. When people asked us why we had come to Israel to help, then we had an opportunity to share our faith with them. People who came to Israel with nothing cried when they heard that complete strangers wanted to serve them, for no reason other than the love of Jesus.

Philip's actions centuries ago might have seemed stupid or irresponsible when he obeyed the Spirit's direction. But he knew it was God, and his obedience caused widespread change. And we can see the ripple effect in our own day because he acted in stark raving obedience. Isn't that what you want for your life, to have an impact that lasts hundreds of years? If you listen to God's voice and obey, the results are supernaturally powerful, even if you don't see them in your lifetime.

People like Abraham, Noah, and Philip must have built a relationship with God beforehand, an established legacy of blessing and miracles through listening to the voice of the Holy Spirit and obeying. The Bible says that God will not put us through trials too hard for us to bear, but He will make us uncomfortable and stretch our faith.

It will start out small. But even the small stuff can feel really uncomfortable. There was one time Dad was driving over to Grand Rapids from our home in Lansing for a meeting. He had a rental car because his car was in an auto repair shop. So as he's driving along, he passes the last exit with a gas station before reaching Grand Rapids, twenty-four miles ahead. A few miles later, he looked down.

The gas gauge read "E." It's not just "E"; it's below "E." And he had never driven this car to know how many miles he really had left in the tank. He didn't have a clue if empty meant *empty* or if it meant "we have about a gallon of fumes left." Now, he found himself neck deep in stress because he was headed to a very important business meeting. If he turned around, he would have been late. If he went forward, he would probably run out of gas and miss the meeting altogether. To him, this was critical. Then it struck him, "Oh, I'll ask God, of course!"

Still driving, he asked, "Do I have enough gas in here to make it to the next exit with a gas station?" In his spirit, he heard, "Yes."

Now, even though he had faith enough to ask God, did he believe what God had just told him in his spirit? Of course not. Any fool could have seen that he didn't have enough gas to make it. So he asked again, "Okay, God. Do You see on this gas gauge where it's not just at 'E,' but *below* 'E' and it is not just below 'E' but way below 'E'? Do I really have enough gas to make it to the meeting?"

"Yes."

Now he had confidence in the still small voice, right? Wrong. He was totally certain that there wasn't enough gas to make it to his exit, and he still argued with God. "Okay. God, if I got off the highway at this little side road and go a few miles north, I would only be a little late for my meeting and I might be able to make it to that gas station . . ." He asked again, "Do I really have enough gas to get to 28th Street?" And then, in his spirit he heard, "Do you trust Me?" In other words, "Do you trust Me more than what you see? Do you trust Me more than the circumstances? Do you trust Me more than the symptoms? If I say it, do you believe it?"

Dad didn't like that answer. He felt a little ashamed, but he kept on rationalizing. "Okay, God. I think I'm an idiot, but You told me to keep going because I have enough gas to make it. But when I run out of gas, then I assume that You're going to bring someone to me that I can share Christ with, it will be a divine appointment and some other thing will happen because I *know* I don't have enough gas . . ." So, white-knuckled, he continued to drive. He got off the highway on his exit ramp, turned the corner into the gas station, and as the front tires hit the entrance of the station, the car started sputtering. It rolled up to the pump and STOPPED! So Dad, all six feet and five inches, jumped out of the car and yelled, "Yes, yes, yes! Jesus, that is so cool," and the guy at the next pump gave him a look and said, "Dude, it's just gas."

But you see, it's not just gas, not when it's building a relationship with the God of the universe. He's going to stretch you. It's going to be a small step, but it'll stretch you and your faith will grow. I know it's going to be uncomfortable. Every time He stretches me, it makes me squirm, and I think, "God, this is getting old!" But He takes me a little farther yet, and I know I have to trust Him. I would rather He just sort of gave me everything (you know, a onetime forty-year supply, and if I act now, I also get the travel-pack knife set), and I didn't have to worry about it, and I could just bless and praise Him with money in the bank and no problems. He's trying to build my character though, and mold who I am into the image of Christ. Bringing up that old cliché about diamonds, time and pressure are a part of the process.

In Matthew 17:24-27, some tax collectors from the temple ask Peter, one of Jesus' disciples, if Jesus plans on paying the temple tax. This put Peter in an awkward situation. Jesus hasn't yet paid the tax, and He's about to get all of their butts audited. Peter goes to Jesus and asks Him about it. Jesus tells Peter, "go to the sea and throw in a hook, and take the first fish that comes up; and when you open its mouth, you will find a shekel. Take that and give it to them for you and Me." Doesn't that strike you as odd? I would have thought that Jesus had gone out of His mind. But what did Peter do? He obeyed. That is stark raving obedience.

And so is this . . .

"Do you have Bibles?"

Clive Culver, former head of World Relief, spoke at Mars Hill Bible Church a couple of years ago and told this story.

Clive was in Iran on a trip visiting some underground pastors and churches. A pastor shared with Clive what had recently happened to his church through God's direction. They had a few Bibles come in, and they wanted to deliver them to a house church in a mountain village outside of Tehran, Iran. So they boxed the Bibles up, put them in a car, and asked a couple of young men to deliver them.

It's sort of dangerous to drive around Tehran in broad daylight with the back of your car loaded with Bibles, since the government there puts you in jail for that type of activity, so they left at five in the morning the next day to make the journey. As they traveled through the city they came to a spot where the car seemed to break. The steering wheel made a hard right turn, and they went slamming around a corner and hit a curb. They thought something major in the front end had snapped.

As they got out to inspect the car, a man approached them. He asked them if they had Bibles. They did not know him and were not about to share information regarding illegal material with a complete stranger. They talked a little about the car and kept on looking for the problem. The man once again, this time more forcefully, asked them, "Where are the Bibles?" This time one of the young men carefully asked him why he would think that they had Bibles.

He said, "I am part of a small house church up the mountain on the other side of Tehran, and we do not have a Bible. It makes it very hard to learn more about Jesus. We asked God to give us a Bible. Last night I had a dream that an angel came and told me if I would come down to this corner at 5:00 this morning that the Lord would give me Bibles. It is 5:00, you have Bibles."

The young men said, "yes we do."

Because that mountain villager listened and obeyed, the request of his house church was fulfilled supernaturally in a land where following Jesus can lead to death. And on top of that, it increased the faith of the young men transporting the Bibles.

When God calls you to do something, and then you do it, what does He do? He blesses you with provision, joy, and peace. Most importantly, He fills your life in every corner with His presence, because *now* you're living the life He always intended for you. Close, intimate, heart-to-heart, friend-to-friend.

You will have also shared your relationship with God to others, like those young men did with the man from the Tehran house church.

Eventually, God will bring you to a point where loved ones might lecture you on responsibility, where the people around you think that you're out of your mind. Some of these people might break off their relationship with you.

I know in my own family that girlfriends, fiancés, family members, and close friends have said or done these things to us. It hurts very much, more than I can say. At that point, though, we had to remember all of the times that God had proved Himself before.

He'll ask you, "Do you trust me?" and you'll probably hate it. I encourage you to follow through anyway. Push through the doubt and discomfort and obey. If you have a question, ask for confirmation, and He will give it to you.

What if Noah decided that he didn't want to give up his time, energy, and pride to build a gigantic boat miles from the sea? Do you have to build an ark in your backyard? I don't know, but I do know that you will have adventures together with God when you listen and obey.

CHAPTER 7

Authority and Healing

Wholeness

As my family grew in our relationships with God, we began to individually ask, "What do You want me to do?" He began to reveal places in our hearts that needed to be reconciled. We found that, through obedience to His guidance, He healed us emotionally and spiritually. He wanted intimacy and restoration more than hired hands.

Also, when sick people asked for prayer, our prayers shifted from "God, if it's Your will, please heal this person of this disease or condition," to "God, how do You want me to pray for this person?"

Soon, He led us to *speak* healing, to pray in ways very different from our normal, familiar prayers. God moved, and He healed people. Now we've come to the point where God has healed and restored thousands of people. We see healings and miracles every week. It's amazing.

One example of this is a woman from a small group that used to meet with my parents. She had developed a kidney disease that caused the organs to deteriorate from the inside. The doctors wanted to operate, but then discovered that the condition of her blood pressure might make the surgery fatal. Without the surgery, though, she would die.

She asked the small group to pray for her, and while they silently prayed, Dad asked God, "How do you want me to pray for her?" He heard the Lord answer, "Ask her these two questions." So when the group began telling the woman what they received in prayer, Dad asked her two questions he felt God place in his mind. "Do you believe that God can heal you?" She said yes. "Okay, do you believe that He will heal you right now?" Without a moment's hesitation she said, "Yes." Then he said, "Well, Father God, You told me to ask the questions, so in the name of Jesus let it be done to her according to her faith." That's all he said. He never actually prayed for her healing.

The next morning, the doctor had X-rays taken before surgery, and he came out shaking his head. "I can't explain this, but the X-rays show that your kidneys are fine. There's nothing wrong with you, go home."

When we heard the news, we rejoiced at what God had done. There were no feelings of self-congratulation because we first asked the question, "God, how do we do this?" We listened, we obeyed, and the blessing chased us down and ran us over.

Marge's Heart

An eighty-eight-year-old woman named Marge came to "W" because God had healed her grandson during one of our meetings. She wanted prayer for her heart valve, which was 98 percent blocked. The hospital would not schedule her for surgery due to other health problems and her age. I joined a group of people, and we prayed with her.

While we prayed for this healing, I heard in my spirit, "Rise up and walk!" I thought, *No way! You're not actually asking me to have this woman get out of her wheelchair, are you?* I mean, this dear lady had been in her wheelchair for years. She faced a life-or-death situation and had just been crying with her husband, Leo. It just, you know, didn't seem like a good time. I felt awkward and didn't want to say it, but the Holy Spirit persisted.

Instead of boldly walking over to Marge and speaking what I heard, I grabbed my friend Tina for backup. We took Marge aside and told her what we were going to pray. She said, "Do you know how old I am?" I shook my head, and she paused. Then she said, "I guess it doesn't matter, does it?" I told her about how Moses, at the age of 120, climbed up the mountain to see the Promised Land before he died (Deut. 34:1-7). God didn't have an age-cap on health or healing. So Tina and I prayed for her legs to strengthen so that she could walk.

Well, Marge didn't jump out of her seat or anything. She thanked us, and I returned to my seat. I thought, *All right, next week, maybe she'll just walk in.* Next week came, and Leo pushed her through the door in her wheelchair. My heart sank a little. I thought, *God, You know what's going on, and I don't need to know.* After worship, when Dad usually asks people for stories of God moving in their lives, Marge motioned for the microphone.

"I haven't been able to walk at all in years, but after you prayed for me, I went home and thought, *I wonder if that worked.* So I got out of my seat and walked the length of my house and back. When I sat down, I thought, *Did I really just do that?* So I did it again, and I've been doing it all week." Although (I later found out) she used a walker to get around on her feet, it still doesn't diminish the miracle in my opinion. Her body was *more* restored, not less.

She went on with her testimony. When she went to the doctor for the heart valve, he ordered a preliminary X-ray. After a while, the doctor came back and said, "I want to show you both of these so you know I'm not lying to you. Here's the X-ray we took last week. See that black spot there? That's where your valve was blocked. And this is the X-ray we just took. There's no black spot. And your heart sounds great. It's as if you have new valves. I can't explain this, but I guess we're done here. You can go home." Sound familiar?

After Marge told us this story, she asked, "I've got arthritis, do you think we could pray for that too?"

Dad responded with one of his favorite jokes, "No, sorry, only one miracle per person."

Again, I was in the group that prayed with her. We listened and asked God how to pray. After a few minutes, Leo remembered a statement that he had made decades before (they had been married almost seventy years at that time). He made a comment about another woman who had a weight problem. This had hurt Marge's feelings and was an indirect assault on her beauty due to her own weight issues. We asked Leo to repent of harming his wife's impression of her beauty and asked Marge to repent of accepting the lie related to her self-worth. Then we prayed and spoke to the arthritis, telling it to leave her body.

Soon afterwards, she reported to us that the arthritic pain had disappeared.

While I was on tour, I got a phone call from Dad. Leo and Marge were walking together in their home when she said, "I think I'm going to fall." Leo caught her and laid her on the floor. She died on the way down. God called her home, and she was walking when it happened.

I learned that two weeks prior to this, Marge had thrown away her prescription heart medications. She told her doctor that there was no more need for them. After all, the X-ray had shown that she had new heart valves. However, since no one performed an autopsy, we can't say for sure what caused her death. What we do know is that God gave Marge and Leo two additional years together, and Marge's health improved dramatically during that time.

I'm adding this little footnote to the story of Marge because I want to make something clear. Dad and I never tell anyone to stop seeing doctors, throw away medication, or refuse surgery. We believe that God gave doctors their knowledge and talent. There are some instances where we've prayed for the doctors to have wisdom, or to find the medical cause of an illness, or to perform the surgery without any complications. Sometimes, we know, God works miracles within the world of medicine.

We also know there is that one-in-one chance of dying. At some point, we're going to die. We pray for people to be healed because we want to see God restore someone who is suffering. We pray because Jesus told His disciples to pray for the sick and oppressed in Matthew 10:1. It serves as a reminder that God is real and wants to be involved in our lives. We don't pray because the Holy Spirit is some sort of righteous life-support system.

Multiple Sclerosis

Five years ago, our church held a series of meetings where people could come for healing prayer. We met for four weeks straight. Dad helped by praying for people and instructing the prayer team. When people came for prayer, Dad stood by and anointed them with oil. Our pastor came down with a bug before the final session and asked

Dad to lead at the last minute.

During the prayer time, a woman named Julie Benison approached Dad. As she struggled to walk toward him, he heard the thought, *self hate.* Now, having never met this person, not knowing her issues, he knew that God was directing how to pray and it made him uncomfortable. She told him that she had Multiple Sclerosis and almost did not come forward because it was so difficult to walk.

We had recently learned that Multiple Sclerosis is an autoimmune disease which causes the body to form holes around the Mylan sheaths protecting the nerves. Many autoimmune diseases (where the body attacks itself) are rooted in self-hate. But how do you say this to a stranger coming to you in need? Just as the Spirit guides. He asked, "As far as you know, is there anything in your past that would cause you to hate yourself?"

Julie gave him a puzzled look and said, "Not that I'm aware of." He told her about the possible root of MS and asked her to pray by herself in the corner. "Ask God to reveal anything in your past that may have caused you to hate yourself. If nothing comes to mind, that's fine. I'll pray for you regardless of what you hear." She agreed and went over to a quiet spot in the room.

A few minutes later, she returned with tears streaming down her face. God reminded her of the self hate she had in her life. Dad had her pray a prayer of repentance for any agreement with self hate. Then he anointed her with oil and called for a creative miracle to restore the Mylan sheaths surrounding her nerves.

Julie later wrote us an email with a copy of her written testimony. After giving the history of her illness, she gave her perspective of the night that God healed her MS.

Eventually, the side effects of the drugs became too much to bear, given the two toddlers in my care. Together, Jim (my husband) and I decided to stop treatment, and take all the good time available to us without the debilitating side effects. Don't get me wrong. MS is not a fatal disease like some cancers, or HIV. This thing would not kill me, just make me unable to do things like walk, use the bathroom normally, play at the park with my kids, clean the house (I don't like that one anyway), hold a glass or mug, etc.

The last time I felt a relapse coming on, I came out to a healing service at Mars Hill. We had been attending for about a year and I knew prayer was the only "treatment" I would happily embrace. Not that we had neglected praying about my health up to that point, quite the contrary. I have two grandmothers (two grandfathers while they were alive) and the most faithful praying mother and father in the world who prayed daily for me—in fact, they'd been doing that daily since December 30, 1970. My husband and I begged God for healing. This is one of the many things I do not understand about the goodness of God. Through all of the fear, depression, numbness, and all that, I knew God was still good. And, He was still good to me. But, because of the prayers of the people God used that night, I walked out of the church with 99% feeling restored in all my parts. But more importantly, I had feeling restored to my soul. The things that were said to me, through me, and by me had more power than the doctors, more power than the psychologists and social workers and support groups. These were the things God used to heal my broken spirit. God counts me as one of His "glorious ones in whom is all my delight" (Psalm 16:3 NIV). The drugs prescribed could not heal old wounds of self-hatred, but God did. His love healed not only my body, but also the pain of my heart that I had buried deep—but not too deep for God's light.

I can count only on one hand any vague symptoms that have flared up in the last year and a half, and when my hand has tingled, I remind it that God took care of that and He clears the nerve-misfire away.

Three years later, her neurologist told her to stop coming for check-ups. There wasn't any point. There were no more signs of Multiple Sclerosis in her body. It has now been seven years and Julie is still free from MS.

Praise God who heals hearts as well as bodies. I have no doubt that Julie still struggles with sin and brokenness like everyone else, and I haven't seen her walk around on air with a halo over her head. The point is that now she has had an experience with the living God, and she can see that the God of the universe wants to have a real heart-to-heart relationship with her. When we come close to God, He begins to heal us and restore us to the way He meant for us to live.

These stories build trust in God's promises. Dad used Julie's story three years ago when he spoke at a prayer and healing conference in New Jersey for the Reformed Church of America. One of the pastors in attendance had come with his wife. She had suffered with MS for more than twenty-seven years, the last seven years in a wheelchair. Julie's story encouraged her to ask for prayer at the end of the conference. It was a simple prayer, and her husband wheeled her out afterwards. It didn't appear that anything had happened.

A year later, we heard from an acquaintance of this pastor. The day after Dad had prayed for this woman, she felt remarkably better. The MS had vanished. She got out of her wheelchair and began to minister alongside her husband again.

Do you see the ripple that a simple act of obedience has? If Dad had dismissed the thought regarding self hate, would Julie have been healed? I don't know. What I do know is that regardless of his discomfort, he obeyed God's direction and Julie is healed. And I know that her testimony encouraged another woman to trust in God's ability to heal. *And* I know that this other woman no longer has MS because of the Lord who heals.

Early on in the history of the "W" service, a woman asked us to pray for her hearing. She had 80 percent hearing loss in one ear. Three days after we prayed for her, she felt a warm pop in the damaged ear and heard clearly again.

A year later, my friend Josh asked for prayer regarding the same hearing problem. Forty-five minutes later, as he drove home from the service, he called me. "I just wanted to let you know that I felt a pop in my ear and felt some stuff drain out. I can hear perfectly out of that ear again."

Praying in authority does not make us "Faith Healers," and it wouldn't necessarily make you a faith healer either. It's not like we're lining up people, knocking them over, and waving white handkerchiefs on cable television. We pray for people, trusting in the words we read from Scripture, acting in obedience to the Spirit's voice, and God moves. We've seen God move too many times to ignore it. I've also seen people remain sick or get worse. Why is it that God seems to heal some people but not others? Why was Josh healed in forty-five minutes and the woman with the same hearing problem healed after three days? Why was Hank healed instantly of cancer, but other people had their tumors shrink over a period of time? I have come up with a good and biblically sound answer for these questions: I don't know.

God probably doesn't need me to defend Him. I'm not trying to prove the credibility of the things that have happened. I just know that they have happened. I choose to bless God when people are healed and ask for understanding when they are not. I do not own the result either way.

Is it God's will to heal?

There are three core elements to our understanding of healing: it is God's will to heal, belief impacts the result, and we need to understand and operate in the authority God gave us through Jesus, His death, and His resurrection.

When I began to understand the reality of this, I changed the way I prayed. I went from praying and hoping that people would be healed (which seldom happened) to now seeing hundreds of people healed. Dad has seen thousands healed.

First, it *is* God's will to heal. The Bible is true. I know that men wrote the words, and that there are cultural contexts here, there, and everywhere, but I believe that God's truth is in every word. I firmly, deeply believe this. I have based my whole life around the truth that I read in it. So, when I read Psalm 103:2-3 "Bless the LORD, O my soul, and forget none of His benefits; who pardons all your iniquities, who heals all your diseases," I believe that He forgives my sin and heals my body. And when I read Isaiah 53:5 where it says that by Jesus' wounds we are healed, I really believe that Jesus also died on the cross to take on the burden of sickness. Mental distress, emotional suffering, and disease are all products of sin, the Fall and the curse which came into the world when Adam and Eve decided that they didn't need to listen to God's command. Jesus came to free us from sin and every other part of the curse, so I believe that means Jesus freed us from all the *products* of sin and the curse as well. Why would God want to only restore portions of us?

It might help to look at what Jesus believed about God's will regarding healing. Read the first part of Matthew 8. In verse 2, a leper comes to Jesus and makes this statement, "If You are willing . . ." How does Jesus respond? He says, "I am willing. Be cleansed." And this man's skin was immediately cleansed.

One interpretation of the phrase "I am willing" is "*Of course* I am willing." Is God willing to heal and cleanse us? Of course, He says. The word shows us that Jesus healed all who came to Him and believed. A large part of the Western church today doesn't believe that this still happens. It's my conviction that if a church says that they believe the Bible, they can't pick what parts of the Bible they want to believe. When someone says that God's supernatural involvement in mankind "was for then, but it doesn't happen now," that's a school of thought called "dispensationalism." As I see it, there is no biblical basis for that statement. I really think that it came from men trying to explain why there was no life or power in their church. Nothing that they say diminishes what I actually see written in the Bible. And the Word of God says that it *is* His will to heal.

Jesus makes another interesting point on healing in John 9. He and His disciples came across a blind man, and the disciples asked, "Rabbi, who sinned, this man or his parents, that he would be born blind?" (v. 2). This was a common belief among the Jewish people at that time. Jesus answered that neither reason had caused the blindness. It was the result of living in a world under a curse of sin, but He said that because of it, God would be glorified. Jesus healed the man and the man praised God, testifying before the religious leaders.

If staying blind would have glorified God, why would Jesus heal this man? The infirmity didn't bring the glory, the healing did.

We can learn and grow in every situation we encounter because God redeems all things in Christ. But I've never seen anything in the Bible where Christ leaves people ill to glorify God. It's the healing that glorifies Him. We don't serve a God of sickness. We serve a God who heals, a God who redeemed us from the sin that caused all of this suffering in the first place.

Over the years, many people have asked, "Doesn't God sometimes want people to be sick? What about the affliction He allowed on Job? What about the 'thorn in Paul's flesh' that God wouldn't take away?"

The "thorn in Paul's flesh" was not an illness. In 2 Corinthians 12, Paul talks about great revelations that God had given him. But he recognized the possibility of taking pride in his knowledge.

> Because of the surpassing greatness of the revelations, for this reason, to keep me from exalting myself, there was given me a thorn in the flesh, a messenger of Satan to torment me—to keep me from exalting myself! Concerning this I implored the Lord three times that it might leave me. And He has said to me, "My grace is sufficient for you, for

power is perfected in weakness." Most gladly, therefore, I
will rather boast about my weaknesses, so that the power
of Christ may dwell in me. (2 Cor. 12:7-9)

The thorn in Paul's flesh was an evil spirit that attacked him.
Paul asked God to keep an evil spirit from attacking him, not to heal
him of an ailment. But God didn't promise that the enemy wouldn't
attack us. That's why Paul spoke of spiritual warfare in Ephesians
6:10-18. There *is* a battle against spiritual forces, and we need to be
aware of how to rely on God in the midst of it.

As for Job, it took me years before I realized that Job's sickness
came as a result of sin. Yes, I know that Job was a righteous man
who sought God and so on. But Job had made agreements with
the subtle lie of fear. While mourning his situation, Job said, "For
what I fear comes upon me, and what I dread befalls me. I am not
at ease, nor am I quiet, and I am not at rest, but turmoil comes"
(Job 3:25-26).

Ultimately, Job did not trust God, and his fear gave Satan the
right to torment him. So, no, I don't find anything in the Bible that
ever says God wants people to remain broken and ill.

Second, our belief impacts the result of our healing. Earlier,
I told you that if your starting point for hearing God is, "I can't
hear God," then you are right. The same goes for healing. If you
say, "it's not God's will to heal," or "He doesn't heal people today,"
then how can you ask God to heal? Those words have no trust in
them, and they are empty. They would not bring a positive result
except by grace. If you do not believe that belief has any impact on
whether a person is healed, then why is it that we have this story in
Matthew 13:55-58?

"Is not this the carpenter's son? Is not His mother called Mary, and His brothers, James and Joseph and Simon and Judas? And His sisters, are they not all with us? Where then did this man get all these things?" And they took offense at Him. But Jesus said to them, "A prophet is not without honor except in his hometown and in his own household." And He did not do many miracles there because of their unbelief.

Because of Unbelief

Not a lack of desire on the part of Jesus. Not a lack of Jesus' ability. He was God, for crying out loud. It didn't come from having "too little faith," but *no belief* to rest any faith upon. The people in Jesus' hometown basically said, "Who does this guy think he is? We know his family, we've seen him grow up. He's from our neighborhood. There's nothing special about that." This attitude hindered God's ability to heal because the people flat-out rejected Jesus.

And again, I'm not telling you that you need certain measurements of faith. Jesus told His disciples that it took faith the size of a mustard seed to move mountains. Mustard seeds are tiny. And that's all it really takes. If a person has faith enough to ask, I believe that's faith enough for God to move.

In Hebrew, the word for "faith" can be translated into "trust." It's true that much of the New Testament was written in Greek, where the words for "faith" and "belief" (*aglapistos* and *apistos*) are more or less interchangeable. Theologian David H. Stern makes the argument, though, that all of the New Testament writers were Jewish men with a predominately Hebrew mind-set. Even Luke, who was born a Gentile, was a proselytized Jew before he converted to

Christianity.[19] In our society, the word "faith" has more relation to the word "hope," which makes me feel like "faith" has no security. There's an otherworldly hope in something unseen and scientifically baffling? Is that the kind of security my soul has in this life?

It comes down to this. Do I trust that God's Word is true? Do I trust God when He speaks to me? Or am I afraid that He's not going to come through for me when I need Him? When it comes to belief, God wants to know, "Do you trust Me?"

Third, we need to understand and operate in the authority God gave us through Jesus, His death, and His resurrection.

Think about this. If we really believe that we are called to be like Jesus, that means that we are also called to minister to the sick and brokenhearted, and heal them. In Matthew 10:1, after Jesus called His disciples, He "gave them authority over unclean spirits, to cast them out, and to heal every kind of disease and every kind of sickness." As His followers, we've been commissioned to carry out Christ's work on earth, which includes healing. Jesus says in Mark 16:17-18, "These signs will accompany those who have believed . . . they will lay hands on the sick, and they will recover."

That Scripture also includes a part about handling venomous snakes, stepping on scorpions, and drinking poison and living to tell about all of it. God wasn't, however, commanding us to find a way to cheat death over and over or giving us a list of neat tricks to prove His existence to people. Rather, if someone sees us supernaturally live through an otherwise fatal situation, it's evidence of God's protection for those who believe. Like when that viper bit Paul in Acts 28:3-6 on the island of Malta.

Jesus wasn't suggesting that the disciples drink poison, smack their lips, wipe their mouths, and then praise God because that's not the point. And even though Jesus did authorize the disciples to heal the sick as a part of their ministry, that isn't the point either.

Healing isn't the point of healing.

God loves us. This lies as the base of everything else. Listening prayer isn't about the listening. It's about hearing God speak, obeying, and building our relationship with Him. Songs are not the point of praise and worship. The music is just one way we express our love and trust in God, just one way we say, "You alone are God, and we will worship You alone." It's not a song, it's a sacrifice. It's one way in which we show our love for God. In this same way, the miracle of healing is not the point of healing, it's one way that God shows us His love.

Think about this. When a person starts to think that sensuality is the point of a relationship, it becomes a perversion. Pornography takes the intimacy and commitment out of sex. In the end, it's selfish and disposable. Take what you need when you need it. And you know what? It never fulfills. It doesn't build the relationship because there *is* no relationship.

Beyond simply relieving a person of an illness or pain, healing should bring praise to God. Here's a story out of Luke.

> While He was on the way to Jerusalem, He was passing between Samaria and Galilee. As He entered a village, ten leprous men who stood at a distance met Him; and they raised their voices, saying, "Jesus, Master, have mercy on us!" When He saw them, He said to them, "Go and show yourselves to the priests." And as they were going, they were cleansed. Now one of them, when

he saw that he had been healed, turned back, glorifying God with a loud voice, and he fell on his face at His feet, giving thanks to Him. And he was a Samaritan. Then Jesus answered and said, "Were there not ten cleansed? But the nine—where are they? Was no one found who returned to give glory to God, except this foreigner?" And He said to him, "Stand up and go; your faith has made you well." (Lk. 17:11-19)

The nine lepers just wanted to have Jesus rid them of the disease. The Samaritan leper on the other hand, realized that God healed him and gave God the glory. It would make sense that this man came closer to God because He would heal him, both a Samaritan and a leper, society's lowest outcast.

Even though the Scriptures don't tell us what happened next in the Samaritan's life, let's suppose that we are in his situation. Both the circumstances of society's attitude about our identity and illness have alienated us. We feel unloved, unwanted, and despised. Then Jesus comes and cleanses us of our disease. All of those lepers in the story probably rejoiced in their healing. Wouldn't you? If healing was the focus of this story, Jesus would not have been so surprised that only one man gave thanks to God. The Samaritan understood that he was healed because God loved him. And when he recognized God's love for him, it strengthened his relationship with God. It built his faith, his trust in God. It allowed for deeper intimacy, and intimacy with God is the whole reason Jesus came to set us free.

CHAPTER 8

Our Relationships
Allowing God's Voice to Build and Restore

n Genesis 11, the people decided that they wanted to build a city with "a tower to heaven." This tower would be a monument of their achievements, and it would unify them, keeping them together geographically. The only problem was that this city and tower symbolized their supposed autonomy, their power of human thought and achievement equaled with God.

God said in verse six, "Indeed the people *are one* and they all have *one* language, and this is what they begin to do; now *nothing* that they propose to do will be withheld from them" (NKJV, *emphasis added*). Because of this, God confused their language. Without a common language, the organizational unity broke down, and the people scattered. This story highlights the strength that people have when they get together with understanding and a common goal.

Scripture, especially the New Testament, places a lot of emphasis on gathering with other believers and sharing your relationship with God with them. In 1 Corinthians 12:12-26, Paul described the church as a body, consisting of several different parts, all important to the whole. And in Philippians 2:2, he writes to the church, "make my joy complete by being of the same mind, maintaining the same love, united in spirit, intent on one purpose." The church should function together in unity to fulfill God's will. Through prayer and listening to God's voice, we begin our journey to know more about God and to know His will for our lives.

I mentioned earlier that God would confirm His words through other believers. We were all created unique, able to understand the heart of God in different ways. When a group gets quiet and asks God to reveal something, a person like Rush might get a picture or vision, another hear a word in their spirit, while someone like Etta has a song running through their head. When the people share what God told them individually, the different responses can (and often do) come together to form a greater picture of what God is trying to say to His children.

A few years ago, the Maranatha Christian Conference Center in Muskegon held a pastors' prayer retreat and invited Dad to teach. Dad led the pastors in a time of listening and writing out what they heard from God. While they were listening together, a Nazarene pastor saw a vision of a huge face smiling through a window. He felt that God had given him this vision, but it seemed so strange. This pastor reluctantly told the group what he saw. During the same prayer time, my mother had received a Scripture reference. She read aloud from Song of Solomon 2:9-10, "My beloved is like a gazelle or a young stag. Behold, he is standing behind our wall, he is looking through the windows, he is peering through the lattice. My beloved responded and said to me, 'Arise, my darling, my beautiful one, and come along.'"

This refreshed the hearts of many weary pastors. God had told them in two ways through two members of the assembly that He pursued them and cherished them as a lover.

The confirmation of God's direction through listening creates unity because we can see that the same God speaks to all of us. This also builds your relationship with God because it will seem less like an intangible voice that you hear faintly in your spirit, and more like a real God that interacts with all of His people. He still speaks, and He still speaks to everybody.

Several years ago, my parents began listening with their small group when they prayed. One couple, the Freelands, usually came but they decided to stay home that day.

Just before the rest of the group began to pray, another man, Jerry, came late. He often found himself frustrated when they prayed because in the first few weeks they had listened as a group, he said he never heard God tell him anything. While praying, Dad heard in his spirit, "Jerry has a word for the Freelands." Dad thought to himself, *That's stupid. Jerry never has a word for anyone.* After they finished, Dad told the group, "I heard that Jerry would have a word for the Freelands."

Jerry looked around and said, "Well, I wasn't going to say this, and I don't know if it means anything to them, but I heard the word 'Paint.'"

It just so happened that the Freelands had stayed home to fast and pray, seeking wisdom about a job situation. Their family needed extra income that a business opportunity promised, but Mrs. Freeland felt such a strong desire to create watercolor paintings that she wondered if God wanted her to continue her career as an artist.

For one reason or another, the Freelands had decided not to tell anyone in the small group about her questions. When Dad called and told them what he and Jerry heard, they started crying. God showed them that He wanted Mrs. Freeland to paint. God showed Jerry that

He does indeed speak. And, well, I guess God showed Dad that he needed to trust Him, and not "Ted—the man of faith and power."

Confirmation of Others

Even men of faith and power need the confirmation of others. In Jeremiah 32, the prophet has heard that Israel and Judah will fall captive to Babylon, and that the Babylonians will devastate the land. But then God tells Jeremiah that the land will one day be restored and taken back by His people. To confirm His promise, God tells Jeremiah that his cousin will come offering to sell a field.

Let me put this into some context. To the Jewish people, this was not just a field, but a portion of the Promised Land. When the Israelites came out of Egypt into the Promised Land, God dictated the precise boundaries and portions to each tribe (read Joshua 14-21). They were given specific pieces of land to care for, and they believed that God entrusted that tract of land to them for eternity. For a person to give up or sell their land was almost unthinkable. It was to give away God's gift and was a sign of bad stewardship (this is why Naboth would not sell Ahab his vineyard in 1 Kings 21:1-3).

The story goes on to say that Jeremiah's cousin did sell his field, and this gave Jeremiah hope. He could trust God's promise for the future of His people.

Look at another layer deeper than this. When believers pray together, asking God to give them wisdom and direction about something, then the only responsibility they have is to listen and obey. The decision-making process goes from "how do we decide who's idea is right?" to "Do we listen and obey what we hear from God?"

Before they both understood how to come to God for guidance, when my mom and dad made decisions, it was a matter of, "This is what I think, this is what you think, and we'll go with the better plan (which by the way is my plan)." At any level of agreement, that kind of process lends itself to friction and strife. What if the "better plan" didn't work? This method would open a door for one of them to blame the other person because their plan failed, and "maybe you should listen to me next time." That kind of behavior hardly builds or preserves unity. Now, when they pray, they both go to God and ask Him, "What should we do? What's Your plan?" Once they have unity and peace regarding the direction they receive, they go on from there. If it doesn't work out the way they thought it would, they can't blame each other for the "failure." All they can do is trust that God is in control and that He has a plan greater than our finite minds can understand.

That last point is important to remember. Even when people do come together to seek God's guidance, that doesn't mean it's going to be completely effortless or have a perfect result.

When I was fourteen, I told my parents that I had back pain. Now, I felt aches and pains in my back before from baseball, backpacks, and having a twelve-pound guitar on my shoulder for several hours a day. But this particular night, the pain was especially sharp. Dad told me to take off my shirt so he could have a look. When they saw my back, my mother said that she felt sick. The spine curved an inch to one side and about one and a half inches to the other side.

I had grown several inches in the previous months. That's adolescence for you, I guess. We figured that my muscles didn't grow as fast as my bones, so they pulled the spine out of place. There was talk of doctors and maybe surgery. The thought of rods in my back for the rest of my life made *me* feel sick.

That Sunday morning at church, an evangelist named Sam Rijfkogel told the congregation that he wanted to pray for healing in the evening service. I said, "Dad, that's me. We're going tonight and God's going to heal my back." And this was at a time when we barely knew or understood miracles. At the evening service, an elderly pastor prayed for me, and within the hour my back was arrow-straight.

Okay, my back was miraculously restored. I went to that service trusting God and was healed. I didn't need surgery or intensive physical therapy. But I did have to stretch my muscles and train my body to readjust to a suddenly straight back. Today, I still visit a chiropractor once in a while, but my back is still straight.

In the same way, I've seen God miraculously restore marriages at the W service, but those couples weren't transformed into perfect people. One husband and wife came to the W saying that they were going to file for divorce. They said that the marriage was irreconcilable, and prayer was the last chance for their relationship. By the next week, they had fallen in love again and decided to work through the difficulties that had built up around them. They recently told us that they still have to seek God's direction on how to deal with old wounds as well as new troubles. They still have to work at their marriage even though God gave them a miracle.

The principle of coming to God for direction, asking God for wisdom, will build and preserve unity in the "body of Christ." If the church would come together and ask God for guidance, then I think we would see a decrease in church division because the actions of the church would be based on God's *rhema* word and not human wisdom. God wants the church to act together as one in Him and live as a testimony of His love. If the church would come together and listen to God's voice, they might live as the people building the tower of Babel, truly united in purpose. Only this time, they would build the kingdom of heaven.

CHAPTER 9

When You Pray

Some Thoughts and Suggestions

I t may seem like I gave you a lot to think about, but nothing to do. I guess that's why I'm writing this chapter. It helps sometimes to have clear direction on how to practically use new information. But I want you to understand that these suggestions are mainly based on my family's journey and what God has revealed to those around us. He speaks differently to different people, just how the person needs to hear.

The one constant in praying like this is silence, listening, and waiting on the Lord. It may feel uncomfortable at first, but I'm asking you to try. The Word says in Jeremiah 29 that if we seek Him, we will find Him. Isaiah 30:21 tells us that we will hear a voice guiding us. I want you to pray and ask God to speak to you by the voice of His Holy Spirit. Make sure to be silent and listen. It may sound like a still, small voice in your inner ear, a thought. It may be a picture or a song. Whatever it is, make sure to write it all down.

In the current forward of Mary Geegh's *God Guides* there is a prayer that I've found very helpful.

In the name of Jesus, according to Matthew 28:18 and

> Luke 10:19-20, I take authority over Satan and his fallen
> angels and command that they be rendered deaf, dumb,
> and blind to my prayers and removed from my presence.
> I place my own voice under subjection to the shed blood
> of Jesus and command that my own thoughts be taken
> captive to the obedience of Christ, according to 2 Cor-
> inthians 10:5. I ask, Father, that only Your Holy Spirit
> will speak to me as I wait on You for wisdom, insight,
> and direction.[20]

Repeat this command when you pray, and again, listen for what
God might say and write it down. You can also pray aloud some of
the scripture that I mentioned before and claim them as truth, such
as James 1:5 and especially 2 Corinthians 10:5.

How do I know it was God?

If you hear something in your spirit, the Word tells us that we can
"test the spirit" (1 Jn. 4:1). We can also test the "fruit" (Mt. 7:15).
In fact, I suggest you do test the voices, especially when you're first
learning how to listen. Remember that not every voice is God. Not
every bird is a duck.

First, of course, if what you heard at all contradicts Scripture,
disregard it. God will not go against His own Word. You can also ask
questions. For example, when I hear something in my spirit that doesn't
sit right, I'll ask, "does that stand as truth before Jehovah God?" Then
I listen for an answer. My friend Tina told me she asks the voice the
question based in 1 John 4:2-3, "Did Jesus come in the flesh?" The
Word says that the enemy will not admit to this, thus proving the
nature of the spirit. If you hear a "yes/no/yes/no" answer in response

to these questions, remember that God does not try to confuse people. He won't try to trick you. This is a sign that the voice came from somewhere else and you shouldn't trust it. Remember John 13:2. If Satan can put a thought in Judas's heart, he can put one in ours.

If you pray and find yourself unsure of what you heard, I also encourage you to pray with other people who are willing to listen for God's direction. Quite often, you'll find that God will confirm what He said to you by what He says to them.

Don't forget to write down what they heard when they tell you their answer. Even if it sounds bizarre the first time you hear it, you never know when God will reveal how the answer He gave them will connect with the answer He gave you.

Again, journaling isn't an assignment for class. Personally, though, I've found that writing down what I hear from God helps me to understand Him better. When you pray, seeking an answer or wisdom about something, you may hear something that doesn't make sense right away. You know, at first glance, it may look less like a blessing and more like nonsense. Just write it down anyway. That way, when something does happen, you can look back in your journal and remember what God has done in your life.

Find someplace where you can pray without distraction. Bring your Bible and journal. Sometimes God will direct me to a verse I don't remember reading, or He'll remind me of something He told me earlier that I want to look up in my journal. Ask God to reveal more of Himself to you. Remember, if you seek Him, you *will* find Him.

Are my ears plugged?

If you are experiencing any trouble in praying or hearing God, ask Him to give you a spirit of wisdom and revelation (Eph. 1:17). Ask

God to show you areas of your life where you may need to repent, whether you are aware of any or not. There could be any number of issues like fear, anger, bitterness, unforgiveness, self hatred, etc., that you need cleaned out. When He reveals something that you've held onto, give it up to Him. Ask Him to show you if there is any sin that you need to take care of in your life. Have other believers pray with you, sometimes another person will receive a word that you need to hear. If God shows you something, repent of agreeing and participating with the lie.

First John 1:9 says that if we confess our sins, He is faithful and just to forgive us our sins, and cleanse us of all unrighteousness. I grew up thinking this applies only to sin, but now I believe that it is much broader. "All unrighteousness" means every part of the curse. Jesus redeemed it all at the cross, so I accept it all. Not just for sin, but also for healing, restored relationships, anything we lost in the Fall.

It's important to ask God to fill you up with the presence of the Holy Spirit to replace the lie. The lies, by the way, will try to come back. You may hear in your head, "you haven't really been forgiven; you haven't really been healed. This is all a joke." Do not believe those voices! You have the authority to silence those voices, taking them captive in obedience to Christ. Reject the lies, and ask for God to fill you with the truth.

Prayer with Each Other

If another person asks you to pray for them, whether the person needs healing or wisdom, ask God how to pray. The Holy Spirit will guide you on what to say and do. Don't dismiss the thought. If you ask and offer prayer, you could see God do some wonderful things. Remember that you have been given authority in the name of Jesus.

Speak the Word, appropriate it, and claim it as truth.

Dad got an email from a man who works as a stonemason. His boss, who wasn't a believer, had burned his hand on the job. The man heard God say, "pray for your boss and call forth new flesh." The guy felt pretty strange but asked his boss if he could pray. The boss agreed. In the email, the man said that what followed was "one of the most bumbling, awkward, inarticulate and sad prayers for healing in the history of healing." He did obey, however, and called forth new flesh. There was no visible change in the boss's hand, but the pain had stopped right away.

The next day at the hospital, the doctors told the boss to expect months of therapy and possible skin grafts due to the severity of the burn. But when they cut away the old, burned skin, they found (to their amazement) new skin already growing underneath. The doctors had never seen anything like it before in a burn case. Three days later the man was playing golf.

The man who wrote this email, who obeyed God's prompt with a self-described "bad prayer," saw a miracle with a man who didn't even believe in God. This wasn't in his small group or at church. And he was very uncomfortable. You will very likely be uncomfortable at first, even with people you love and trust. Push through the discomfort to obey and see what God does.

If you decide to pray and listen for the voice of God, you might learn some things we haven't discussed. If you do, please tell us. We take a lot of pleasure in other believers learning more about their relationship with God. That's one of the reasons why listening prayer is so exciting. The stories continue to build our faith, and we want to learn more. The God of the universe cares enough about one young man's life to send a woman into a 7-Eleven for a headstand. He sent the apostle Philip for a walk so Jewish refugees could have shelter two thousand years later. He provided food to my hungry family.

God is bigger than our understanding, but we still try to understand.

And Then . . .
A Conclusion of Sorts

laise Pascal was an author, scientist, mathematician, inventor, and philosopher. In 1660, Pascal discussed the nature of his faith in God and its correspondence with philosophy and reason in his book, *Pensees*. During his studies, he concluded that discoveries in science and math always led to more questions. He would always find more to seek and learn.[21]

As a follower of Christ, Pascal viewed his understanding of God in the same way. The more he learned about God, the more questions he had regarding the nature of God. To Pascal, God was indeed a big God, infinite and ultimately unfathomable. In searching for truth, he was content to learn what he could understand and praise God for what he could not yet understand.

When I at first began to follow God's voice, I will admit that I thought I had figured out the one big secret to the universe. I finally understood God, and everything else from there on would be a snap. I soon realized that I only knew a small part of the God of the universe. I knew a very real part of Him, and I knew it for myself, but to this day I continue to learn more about God. And I learn in very small steps.

When people begin to listen to the voice of the Holy Spirit, I am excited to watch as they make those same small steps. Hopefully, this book will help you as you begin to grow in the knowledge of God. I'd love to hear about your journey, too. When I get up in the morning and pour my coffee, Dad will sometimes call and read a few emails to me from people who have experienced God through listening prayer. What a way to start the day, right? It always encourages us to hear these testimonies.

Ours is a journey. It's a path that never really ends. In *The Great Divorce,*[22] C. S. Lewis describes a busload of souls that take a trip from a city on the edge of what could be called hell to the edge of what could be called heaven. The very reality of the green plains inflicts pain and discomfort in the ghosts, and the light disgusts many of them.

Of course, this is all an allegory. I don't expect that souls take day trips to the edge of heaven. Or at least, maybe not on a bus. The point is that on the way to heaven, the solid people rejoiced in the journey and what they found along the way. None of them ever claimed to have reached the end of the path. They only continued farther up the path, farther into the mountains.

A group of solid people come from the mountains to meet with the ghosts, and they ask the ghosts to accompany them on their journey toward the city of heaven. Several of the ghosts insist that the journey would be far too painful. The solid people explain that their own ghostly bodies began to harden when they traveled up the mountain path.

Also, just a quick aside, I don't ever remember the solid people lording it over the ghosts that they were solid while the ghosts were without substance.

We should rejoice in the unknown, not because we'll never know it, but because we'll always have the joy of seeking and finding. If the path ended, if heaven really was just a place to go when we die, if God made Himself so completely known that there was no more to discover, would I really be satisfied? Would you? Would we really say, "Well that's the end of that, and what a relief" without saying, "So, what do I do now?"

Eternity goes on without end, which means that eternity is not the end. Those who seek after God will be found by Him, but we don't find Him on our own. When God "meets us along the way," we walk with Him and learn and grow and become more like Him.

I'm saying all of this because I want you to understand that this book really hasn't ended. This isn't over. You may have come to the last page, but the truths go on. And maybe I said something that isn't quite right. I mean, that's possible, isn't it? I'm still learning. You will still learn. Just writing, it took several years and several drafts to get this far, and it's not even that far.

So, no, this isn't the one, authoritative, comprehensive guide to hearing God's voice. I only hope that it is a good guide, that I have helped you to understand that you *can* know God, that God is not silent or far away. I should also remind you that even though my fingers typed these words, I was not your guide into the truth. If something stirred inside of you while you read this book, that wasn't me. That was the Holy Spirit speaking with the *rhema* word. Now I hope that from here, the Holy Spirit begins to guide you as the Spirit will guide me into a deeper relationship with the God who is eternal.

And I thank God that eternity goes on, because I can't wait to see what happens next.

Appendix 1

take Proverbs 18:21 very seriously when it says, "Death and life are in the power of the tongue, and those who love it will eat its fruit." That is, what you or I say aloud have very real results.

Although I have already referenced some of these verses before, the following is a list of healing Scriptures Dotie Osteen, of Lakewood Church in Houston, Texas, recited for deliverance from cancer. A lady in Williamston, Michigan, also said these verses over her body and was healed of cancer.

But again, it isn't just about cancer or colds. God wants to heal all of the effects of sin. That means He wants to heal us emotionally, relationally, spiritually, and so on. These verses apply to that kind of healing as well.

Read, pray, and declare with your mouth that the Word is true and that you trust what God says in it.

Exodus 15:26

And He said, "If you will give earnest heed to the voice of the Lord your God, and do what is right in His sight, and give ear to His commandments, and keep all His statutes, I will put none of the diseases on you which I have put on the Egyptians; for I, the Lord, am your healer."

Exodus 23:25

"But you shall serve the LORD your God, and He will bless your bread and your water; and I will remove sickness from your midst."

Deuteronomy 7:15

The LORD will remove from you all sickness; and He will not put on you any of the harmful diseases of Egypt which you have known, but He will lay them on all who hate you.

Deuteronomy 28:1-14, 61

"Now it shall be, if you diligently obey the LORD your God, being careful to do all His commandments which I command you today, the LORD your God will set you high above all the nations of the earth.

2 All these blessings will come upon you and overtake you if you obey the LORD your God:

3 Blessed shall you be in the city, and blessed shall you be in the country.

4 Blessed shall be the offspring of your body and the produce of your ground and the offspring of your beasts, the increase of your herd and the young of your flock.

5 Blessed shall be your basket and your kneading bowl.

6 Blessed shall you be when you come in, and blessed shall you be when you go out.

7 The LORD shall cause your enemies who rise up against you to be defeated before you; they will come out against you one way and will flee before you seven ways.

8 The LORD will command the blessing upon you in your barns and in all that you put your hand to, and He will bless you in the land which the LORD your God gives you.

9 The LORD will establish you as a holy people to Himself, as He swore to you, if you keep the commandments of the LORD your God and walk in His ways.

10 So all the peoples of the earth will see that you are called by the name of the LORD, and they will be afraid of you.

11 The LORD will make you abound in prosperity, in the offspring of your body and in the offspring of your beast and in the produce of your ground, in the land which the LORD swore to your fathers to give you.

12 The LORD will open for you His good storehouse, the heavens, to give rain to your land in its season and to bless all the work of your hand; and you shall lend to many nations, but you shall not borrow.

13 The LORD will make you the head and not the tail, and you only will be above, and you will not be underneath, if you listen to the commandments of the LORD your God, which I charge you today, to observe them carefully,

14 and do not turn aside from any of the words which I command you today, to the right or to the left, to go after other gods to serve them."

61 "Also every sickness and every plague which, not written in the book of this law, the LORD will bring on you until you are destroyed."

Deuteronomy 30:19-20

"I call heaven and earth to witness against you today, that I have set before you life and death, the blessing and the curse. So choose life in order that you may live, you and your descendants,

20 by loving the LORD your God, by obeying His voice, and by holding fast to Him; for this is your life and the length of your days,

that you may live in the land which the LORD swore to your fathers, to Abraham, Isaac, and Jacob, to give them."

1 Kings 8:56

"Blessed be the LORD, who has given rest to His people Israel, according to all that He promised; not one word has failed of all His good promise, which He promised through Moses His servant."

Psalm 91:16

With a long life I will satisfy him and let him see My salvation.

Psalm 103:3

Who pardons all your iniquities, Who heals all your diseases.

Psalm 107:20

He sent His word and healed them, And delivered them from their destructions.

Psalm 118:17

I will not die, but live, And tell of the works of the LORD.

Proverbs 4:20-23

My son, give attention to my words; Incline your ear to my sayings.
21 Do not let them depart from your sight; Keep them in the midst of your heart.
22 For they are life to those who find them And health to all their body.
23 Watch over your heart with all diligence, For from it flow the springs of life.

Isaiah 41:10

"Do not fear, for I am with you; Do not anxiously look about you, for I am your God I will strengthen you, surely I will help you, Surely I will uphold you with My righteous right hand."

Isaiah 53:4-5

Surely our griefs He Himself bore, And our sorrows He carried; Yet we ourselves esteemed Him stricken, Smitten of God, and afflicted. 5 But He was pierced through for our transgressions, He was crushed for our iniquities; The chastening for our well-being fell upon Him, And by His scourging we are healed.

Jeremiah 1:12

Then the LORD said to me, "You have seen well, for I am watching over My word to perform it."

Jeremiah 30:17

"For I will restore you to health and I will heal you of your wounds,' declares the LORD, because they have called you an outcast, saying: 'It is Zion; no one cares for her.'"

Joel 3:10

Beat your plowshares into swords and your pruning hooks into spears; Let the weak say, "I am a mighty man."

Nahum 1:9

Whatever you devise against the LORD, He will make a complete end of it. Distress will not rise up twice.

Matthew 8:2-3

And a leper came to Him and bowed down before Him, and said, "Lord, if You are willing, You can make me clean."

3 Jesus stretched out His hand and touched him, saying, "I am willing; be cleansed." And immediately his leprosy was cleansed.

Matthew 8:17

This was to fulfill what was spoken through Isaiah the prophet: "HE HIMSELF TOOK OUR INFIRMITIES AND CARRIED AWAY OUR DISEASES."

Matthew 18:18-19

"Truly I say to you, whatever you bind on earth shall have been bound in heaven; and whatever you loose on earth shall have been loosed in heaven.

19 Again I say to you, that if two of you agree on earth about anything that they may ask, it shall be done for them by My Father who is in heaven."

Matthew 21:21

And Jesus answered and said to them, "Truly I say to you, if you have faith and do not doubt, you will not only do what was done to the fig tree, but even if you say to this mountain, 'Be taken up and cast into the sea,' it will happen."

Mark 11:23-24

"Truly I say to you, whoever says to this mountain, 'Be taken up and cast into the sea,' and does not doubt in his heart, but believes that what he says is going to happen, it will be granted him.

24 Therefore I say to you, all things for which you pray and ask, believe that you have received them, and they will be granted you."

Mark 16:17-18

"These signs will accompany those who have believed: in My name they will cast out demons, they will speak with new tongues;
18 they will pick up serpents, and if they drink any deadly poison, it will not hurt them; they will lay hands on the sick, and they will recover."

John 10:10

"The thief comes only to steal and kill and destroy; I came that they may have life, and have it abundantly."

John 3:21-22

"But he who practices the truth comes to the Light, so that his deeds may be manifested as having been wrought in God."
22 After these things Jesus and His disciples came into the land of Judea, and there He was spending time with them and baptizing.

Romans 4:17-20

(as it is written, "A FATHER OF MANY NATIONS HAVE I MADE YOU") in the presence of Him whom he believed, even God, who gives life to the dead and calls into being that which does not exist.
18 In hope against hope he believed, so that he might become a father of many nations according to that which had been spoken, "SO SHALL YOUR DESCENDANTS BE."
19 Without becoming weak in faith he contemplated his own body, now as good as dead since he was about a hundred years old, and

the deadness of Sarah's womb;

20 yet, with respect to the promise of God, he did not waver in unbelief but grew strong in faith, giving glory to God.

Romans 8:11

But if the Spirit of Him who raised Jesus from the dead dwells in you, He who raised Christ Jesus from the dead will also give life to your mortal bodies through His Spirit who dwells in you.

2 Corinthians 10:4-5

For the weapons of our warfare are not of the flesh, but divinely powerful for the destruction of fortresses.

5 We are destroying speculations and every lofty thing raised up against the knowledge of God, and we are taking every thought captive to the obedience of Christ.

Galatians 3:13-14

Christ redeemed us from the curse of the Law, having become a curse for us—for it is written, "CURSED IS EVERYONE WHO HANGS ON A TREE"—

14 in order that in Christ Jesus the blessing of Abraham might come to the Gentiles, so that we would receive the promise of the Spirit through faith.

Ephesians 6:10-17

Finally, be strong in the Lord and in the strength of His might.

11 Put on the full armor of God, so that you will be able to stand firm against the schemes of the devil.

12 For our struggle is not against flesh and blood, but against the rulers, against the powers, against the world forces of this darkness, against the spiritual forces of wickedness in the heavenly places.

13 Therefore, take up the full armor of God, so that you will be able to resist in the evil day, and having done everything, to stand firm.

14 Stand firm therefore, HAVING GIRDED YOUR LOINS WITH TRUTH, and HAVING PUT ON THE BREASTPLATE OF RIGHTEOUSNESS,

15 and having shod YOUR FEET WITH THE PREPARATION OF THE GOSPEL OF PEACE;

16 in addition to all, taking up the shield of faith with which you will be able to extinguish all the flaming arrows of the evil one.

17 And take THE HELMET OF SALVATION, and the sword of the Spirit, which is the word of God.

Philippians 2:13

For it is God who is at work in you, both to will and to work for His good pleasure.

Philippians 4:6-7

Be anxious for nothing, but in everything by prayer and supplication with thanksgiving let your requests be made known to God.

7 And the peace of God, which surpasses all comprehension, will guard your hearts and your minds in Christ Jesus.

2 Timothy 1:7

For God has not given us a spirit of timidity, but of power and love and discipline.

Hebrews 10:23

Let us hold fast the confession of our hope without wavering, for He who promised is faithful.

Hebrews 10:35

Therefore, do not throw away your confidence, which has a great reward.

Hebrews 11:11

By faith even Sarah herself received ability to conceive, even beyond the proper time of life, since she considered Him faithful who had promised.

Hebrews 13:8

Jesus Christ is the same yesterday and today and forever.

James 5:14-15

Is anyone among you sick? Then he must call for the elders of the church and they are to pray over him, anointing him with oil in the name of the Lord;

15 and the prayer offered in faith will restore the one who is sick, and the Lord will raise him up, and if he has committed sins, they will be forgiven him.

1 Peter 2:24

And He Himself bore our sins in His body on the cross, so that we might die to sin and live to righteousness; for by His wounds you were healed.

3 John 2

Beloved, I pray that in all respects you may prosper and be in good health, just as your soul prospers.

Revelation 12:11

And they overcame him because of the blood of the Lamb and because of the word of their testimony, and they did not love their life even when faced with death.

Appendix 2

've listed some books here that have helped my dad and me to understand hearing God's voice and building an intimate relationship with Him. I suggest that you read some of these books as well.

God Guides—Mary Geegh (copies available at www.hearinggod.org)
Dialogue With God—Mark Virkler
Surprised by the Voice of God—Jack Deere
How to Listen to God—Charles Stanley
On Prayer—Andrew Murray
The Joy of Listening to God—Joyce Huggett
Listening for God—Ben Campbell Johnson
The Voice of God—Cindy Jacobs
Listening Prayer—Leanne Payne
In Search of Guidance—Dallas Willard
Prayer: Conversing with God—Rosalind Rinker
Is That Really You, God?—Loren Cunningham
The Lives of the Desert Fathers—translated by Norman Russell
Forever Ruined for the Ordinary—Joy Dawson
Too Busy Not to Pray—Bill Hybels

Listening Prayer—Mary Ruth Swope

A More Excellent Way—Henry W. Wright

Hearing God—Peter Lord

Red Moon Rising—Pete Greig

The Great Divorce—C. S. Lewis

Perelandra (and the rest of the Space Trilogy)—C. S. Lewis

Letters To Malcom—C. S. Lewis

Pensees—Blaise Pascal

The Bondage Breaker—Neil T. Anderson

How Should We Then Live?—Francis Schaeffer

The Prophets—Abraham Heschel

Introduction to the Complete Jewish Bible—David H. Stern

The God Who Is There—Francis Schaeffer

Letters of Francis A. Schaeffer—Lane T. Dennis, ed.

Endnotes

1. David Wilkerson, *Hearing the Voice of God!* 10/17/1988. Permission granted by World Challenge, Inc, P.O. Box 260, Lindale, TX 75771.

2. *The Lives of the Desert Fathers*, translated by Norman Russell, A. R. Mowbray & Co. Ltd, Oxford, 1981.

3. Jack Deere, *Surprised by the Voice of God*, Zondervan Publishing House, Grand Rapids, MI, 1996.

4. A.W. Tozer, *The Pursuit of God - The Pursuit of Man*, Christian Publications, Inc, Camp Hill, PA, 1993, 61.

5. *Surprised by the Voice of God*, 13-17.

6. Taken from *Letters of Francis A. Schaeffer*, edited by Lane T. Dennis, Crossway Books, 1986, 76. Used by permission of Crossway Books, a division of Good News Publishers, Wheaton, IL 60187, www.crossway.com.

7. Mary Audrey Raycroft, *How We Minister & Administer: Are You Hearing or Listening?*, Toronto Airport Christian Fellowship, 1999, www.tacf.org

8. C.S. Lewis *Perlandra*, Scribner, New York, 1996, 120.

9. Mary Geegh, *God Guides*, available at www.hearinggod.org

10. Mark Virkler, *Dialogue with God*, Bridge Publishing, 1986.

11. Andrew Murray, *On Prayer*, Whitaker House, New Kensington, PA, 1998, 340.

12. Neil T. Anderson, *The Bondage Breaker*, Harvest House, 1990.

13. Jason Chatraw, *Closing the Gap: An Interview with Philip Yancey, In Touch*, December 2000.

14. Ray C. Stedman, *How Prayer Works*, Discovery Publishing, Palo Alto, CA, 1995, www.pbc.org.

15. C. S. Lewis, *Letters to Malcolm: Chiefly on Prayer*, Harcourt Brace & Company, Orlando, FL, 1992, 5.

16. Joyce Huggett, *The Joy of Listening to God*, InterVarsity Press, 1986, 169.

17. Jonathan Graf, *The Willing Ear: Responding Obediently to God Voice, Pray!*, Sept/Oct 2001, 13.

18. Francis Schaeffer, *The God Who Is There*, InterVarsity Press, Downers Grove, IL, 1982, 203.

19. David H. Stern, *Complete Jewish Bible*, Jewish New Testament Publications, Inc, Clarksville, MD, 1998, xxxv.

20. Mary Geegh, *God Guides*, introduction.

21. Blaise Pascal, *Pensees*. Recommended reading for anyone and everyone.

22. C. S. Lewis, *The Great Divorce*, Touchstone, New York, 1996.

Contact Ted Kallman

Speaking/Consulting

TED KALLMAN is a well-known speaker at prayer and healing conferences and has also lectured at a large cross section of churches and organizations. Ted and his wife, Claudia, are lay prayer leaders in Grandville, Michigan, where they lead a prayer and healing service every Wednesday evening called the "W."

Ted is available for speaking and conference ministry in your church or community. To contact him regarding questions or to discuss possible speaking engagements:

616-634-2918
ted@i2k.com

Information and many resources are available at his ministry website
www.hearinggod.org.

Ted is also available as a strategic advisor and business consultant. His consulting practice ranges from executive coaching to management and organizational turnarounds. He is the creator and co-author of the Unified Vision Framework which is the basis for an MBA program in project management at Central Ostrobothnia University of Applied Sciences in Kokkola, Finland.

Contact Isaiah

Speaking/Music Ministry

ISAIAH KALLMAN is available to teach on the topics presented in *Stark Raving Obedience*. He can speak to any aged audience, but is very experienced at connecting with 20s and high school students.

He is also available as a music artist or worship leader. He has performed on 33 records, touring the United States for six years. His former band, Vigilantes, appeared in JANE magazine's unsigned artists CD in 2006. He was the worship leader for a large West Michigan church youth group, singing in front of 700 high schoolers a week. He continues to lead worship and performs original material under the name IKAIK.

To contact Isaiah for possible speaking engagements, worship services, or IKAIK performances, please write to:

isaiahkallman@gmail.com

Read more from Isaiah on his weblog:

isaiahkallman.blogspot.com